Margaret Doner

Merlin's War

*The Battle between the Family of
Light and the Family of Dark*

iUniverse, Inc.
Bloomington

Merlin's War
The Battle between the Family of Light and the Family of Dark

Copyright © 2012 Margaret Doner

All rights reserved. No part of this book may be used or reproduced by any means, graphic, electronic, or mechanical, including photocopying, recording, taping or by any information storage retrieval system without the written permission of the publisher except in the case of brief quotations embodied in critical articles and reviews.

iUniverse books may be ordered through booksellers or by contacting:

iUniverse
1663 Liberty Drive
Bloomington, IN 47403
www.iuniverse.com
1-800-Authors (1-800-288-4677)

Because of the dynamic nature of the Internet, any Web addresses or links contained in this book may have changed since publication and may no longer be valid. The views expressed in this work are solely those of the author and do not necessarily reflect the views of the publisher, and the publisher hereby disclaims any responsibility for them.

Any people depicted in stock imagery provided by Thinkstock are models, and such images are being used for illustrative purposes only.

Certain stock imagery © Thinkstock.

ISBN: 978-1-4759-0658-5 (sc)
ISBN: 978-1-4759-0660-8 (hc)
ISBN: 978-1-4759-0659-2 (e)

Printed in the United States of America

iUniverse rev. date: 4/12/2012

Acknowledgements

I wish to thank all my friends and clients who have given me so much support and love throughout the years. My husband, Chris, is the reason I have the strength to continue with this work. My dear friend, Jamie, helped me edit and kept me strong as well when I felt doubt. To those who read the material and watched it grow I am deeply grateful for your input. Thanks Karen for your assistance!

And last but not least, to those who have shared sacred journeys with me, I am thankful for your friendship. Together we liberate ourselves and others.

The book is dedicated to all the whistleblowers, innovators and leaders who have given their lives to see the planet Earth and humanity liberated from prison. It is dedicated to those who work each day to bring more Light and Truth to this planet. For hundreds of years these brave souls have spoken their truth in the face of darkness and fear.

PART I *The Battle Between the Family of Light and the Family of Dark*   1

MERLIN: THE BEGINNING	5
VLAD DRACULA RESPONDS	11
MERLIN: CREATION EVOLVES	13
VLAD DRACULA: THE DINOSAURS	16
MERLIN: EVOLVING THE DINOSAURS	18
VLAD DRACULA: THE LIE OF CAMELOT	26
MERLIN: VLAD THE IMPALER	29
VLAD DRACULA: I AM THE TRUE LEADER	31
MERLIN: JESUS AND VLAD	34
VLAD DRACULA: I TOO AM PART OF THE LIVING GOD	38
MERLIN: HOW THE BATTLE HAS BEEN WAGED – THE LUCIFERIAN DECEPTION	39
VLAD DRACULA: I ONLY CREATED BY MERLIN'S RULES	44
MERLIN: THE ORION WARS CONTINUE	46
VLAD DRACULA: WHY THE QUARANTINE WAS ENACTED	49
MERLIN: THE GAME OF LIFE	50
VLAD DRACULA: MERLIN AS THE EVIL GOD	54
MERLIN: FALLEN ANGEL GODS	56
VLAD DRACULA: MY CASE AGAINST THE PLEIADIANS	61
MERLIN: WHAT HE DIDN'T STEAL HE DESTROYED	63

VLAD DRACULA: THE CENTAURS	66
MERLIN: THE FALLEN ANGELS AND BETELGEUSE	68
VLAD DRACULA: THE DEMONICS	72
MERLIN: VLAD DRACULA AND THE NAZI AGENDA	73
VLAD DRACULA: MEMBERS OF THE FAMILY OF LIGHT ARE WHINING BABIES	81
MERLIN: MORE ON THE NEPHILIM	84
VLAD DRACULA: HACKING INTO THE MATRIX	87
MERLIN: ESCAPING FROM THE MATRIX	91
VLAD DRACULA: MATRIX PROGRAM #10	94
MERLIN: THE EXPANSION OF CREATION	96
VLAD DRACULA: THE TIME AND SPACE MATRIX PROGRAMS	99
MERLIN: WHAT ARE YOU GOING TO DO ABOUT IT?	102
VLAD DRACULA: I AM THE DRAGON GOD	105
MERLIN: THE TEMPLATE WAR	107
VLAD DRACULA: CREATION OF THE TITANS and ANTAREANS	112
MERLIN: ROBOTS AND THEIR INFLUENCE ON EARTH	114
VLAD DRACULA: THE WAR ON MARS	118
MERLIN: STONEHENGE AND VLAD DRACULA	122
VLAD DRACULA: STONEHENGE THE BATTLE	124
MERLIN: THE NEANDERTHALS AND THE ET BLOODLINES	125

VLAD DRACULA: GLADIOUS THE NEANDERTHAL	127
MERLIN: THE END OF DAYS AND REVELATIONS	128
VLAD DRACULA: THE END OF DAYS	130
MERLIN: COPING WITH THE WAKE-UP CALL	131
VLAD DRACULA: UNDERSTANDING THE DARK MIND	136
MERLIN: THE RETURN OF CYGNUS – THE WHITE DRAGON	139

PART II *The Human Journey: My Journey*   **141**

PART I
The Battle Between the Family of Light and the Family of Dark

This information is not given to you as Truth, but to stimulate the truth that lies within you. Only you can decide what truth is for you. That is what makes you Masters and not victims.

I have been working as a channel for the angelic realm for many years and I am the author of *Archangels Speak*, and *Wisdom of the Archangels*. In 1996 I became a certified past life regression therapist, having trained with Roger Woolger, PhD, and have had the great good fortune to assist many people to remember and integrate lives not only on this planet, but also on other planets. I have also aided those who suffered from alien abduction trauma to heal from fear and reclaim their soul fragments. Through these experiences I have come to understand, at much deeper levels, the drama that is being played out on the planet Earth, the drama that many people refer to as the battle between good and evil.

Like so many I have become aware of an enormous amount of assistance the human race receives from both extraterrestrial and extradimensional beings. Whether they are Pleiadians, Arcturians, and Andromedans, or Archangel Michael, Gabriel and Raphael, these beings are available to help those of us willing to seek them out. Many of us relate to these beings as "family," and we call them the Family of Light. Simultaneously I have also become aware of a force of resistance that many of us encounter as well. This oppositional force we call the Family of Dark. It is my intention, in this book, to give voice to leaders from these opposing families; Merlin who represents the Family of Light and Vlad Dracula who represents the Family of Dark.

Merlin is thought of by most humans as a simple embodiment of the wizard. In this book he is much more. He is a powerful Creator God who is responsible for creating the human template and seeding life on the Earth. Dracula is thought of as a simple vampire. In this book he is much more. He is the being we call Satan, and he is responsible for creating war and chaos on Earth and in other galaxies.

The one thing both these beings agree on is that the human race has been completely unaware of its own reality. According to Merlin the history of the human race has been manipulated by a being so clever, so "in the background," that human beings have had no idea he exists. In fact, he has hidden behind Lucifer, but Lucifer is not your devil. Merlin wishes you to understand the battle he has waged with the being you call Dracula, the being who really is the devil. Most people are aware that there lived an actual historical figure named Vlad Dracula or Vlad the Impaler. As a past life therapist I have removed the energetic residue of his impalement stakes from many clients, not only freeing the physical body from pain but helping to free my client's emotional body from the fear that Dracula's gruesome death imprinted upon them.

Dracula believes that Merlin is at fault and that he is the rightful ruler of all creation. Dracula believes that his creation, the reptilians, are superior, and he has set out to prove this to Merlin and to all of us. So, presented here are two points of view, and to be fair I have agreed to tell both sides.

It is my belief that without both points of view there would be no truth, for as always truth is held in the consciousness of the beholder. To find truth you must look at all sides of an issue. The world has been polarized for too long, and it is my intention to serve as a bridge between the Family of Light and the Family of Dark and assist them to find harmony. Do not treat this as your Truth, but utilize it to stimulate the truth within you. Only when you can look at the other side without fear can you become empowered. It is time for the playing field to be evened out. The Family of Dark has been in control for too long, and it's time for the Family of Light to climb out of the fear that has kept them enslaved.

Fear creates the shadow that blocks love—love releases us from fear. Not love, but Love. Love that is so all encompassing it is capable of holding both dark and light in its embrace.

MERLIN: THE BEGINNING

What follows is channeled material. It has been gathered directly from Merlin and Vlad. I receive my information through "knowing," not by hearing voices. Dracula's intentions were allowed to be known to me; but I was protected from direct contact with his energy during the writing of this book.

This book is designed to provoke. It is also designed to stimulate you to define your own beliefs about the nature of good and evil. As a teacher this is Merlin's style. He will challenge you to state your truth in what might appear (to some) as confrontational ways. In other words, sometimes Merlin believes you get to your own truth faster by disagreeing with someone than by agreeing with them. He feels that this approach forces the student to declare who they are and as a result enables them to climb into their own mastery.

The following material expresses multi-dimensional reality by blending what some would consider fiction with what others consider truth. Again, that is up to you to decide. It is a dialogue between Dracula and Merlin and it tells the story of their war and its impact upon all of us.

There was no fall. Not as you have been told. Nobody got kicked out of heaven by God; but many beings created hell. There is a difference. Forget everything you think you know. Forget it. It hasn't served you, and it has misled you. Be willing to let go of everything. What do you know? What knowledge is your knowledge; inherent within you? You have never owned anything except your feelings.

Everything else you have either read in books, been told in church, by your parents, or your government. What do you really know?

Once upon a time you knew the world was flat. Now you know it's round. But, you don't. You know nothing about outer space or about the Earth. Even today there are those who believe that the Earth is hollow, and there are entrances into the inner Earth at both ends, and portals into the inner Earth at various "power points." They will swear that the Earth contains a sun inside—a light source of great magnitude—and strange creatures live within the Earth. There are those who will swear that is the talk of dreamers and idiots. This is happening right here and now. This is your home planet, and you still don't all agree where you live. Not even close.

So, here I am to tell you another story. A story that shakes everything you've been told. For some of you it will resonate as truth, and to others it will appear fiction. The choice is yours, of course.

Let us begin at what I am going to call, for convenience sake, the beginning. God. None of us know what's before God. So, it is as good a place to start as any. For the romantic souls I will say God impulsed Love and created life. For those with cruder tastes I will say God belched. Your scientists call it the Big Bang. Did God perceive himself, and then react in response to the perception; or did God react and then perceive himself? That is up to you to decide. What came first, the chicken or the egg? Either way it was when God perceived himself that consciousness became aware of creation. In the beginning creation was innocent. It was free floating particles of energy bubbles. That level of creation is pretty uninteresting so I won't waste words on that. Soon enough, however, the energy bubbles began to coalesce and the act of one "bubble" uniting with another "bubble" created enough "other" that true awareness began. You see, awareness cannot begin until there is an "other" to compare the self to. It's as if you don't know you exist until you see another, and when the other becomes evident you know there is a you.

In the beginning consciousness was content to gaze at the other, and at the self, and merely to experience the new sensation of "other" and "me." But as more and more of these bubbles began to merge, and more and more of them began to gain this new level of awareness, *The Source of Creation* became self aware. God gazed upon these bubbles and noticed them; She was aware that they were both her and not her. (God will be referred to in both the masculine and feminine in order to remain gender neutral.) "Is this me?" asked God.

Early on the bubbles began to take more and more sophisticated shape. In the beginning was the Word. What that means is that in the beginning pure consciousness (or vibration) created reality—and instantly. A bubble would bump into another bubble, and feel the presence of that bubble, which would stimulate consciousness, and creation would take place. Suddenly there is the awareness of a long oblong bubble, and creation is on its way.

As creation became more and more sophisticated, the angelic realm emerged. The angelic realm is the realm closest to God or the Source, closest to pure creational energy, yet still self-aware and differentiated. Self-awareness grew among the angels. They began to develop what you would call personalities. The angelic world was simple in the beginning, but gaining quickly in sophistication, because the angelic world, in its earliest stages, was quite co-operational. They hadn't yet discovered conflict. Perhaps it would be best for me to suggest the idea of cherubs. The earliest beings were cherubs. The baby angels, if you will.

Cherubs were the first ones to discover how to play with the bubbles, and create things with them. They enjoyed playing with the bubbles and making shapes. They began creation by moving this energy called God into form. Even today this is true; cherubs take the energy directly from God and move it outward so that other beings, called Creator Gods, can make more and more sophisticated creations from the energy.

God doesn't create directly. God supplies the energy of creation and is aware of the creations made from His energy; but God does not mold the energy himself. She passes it on, or belches it out, and allows us to create with it. Play with it. Express ourselves with it. We are all God, of course. Where else would we come from? As Gods yourselves you are given the opportunity to create reality, and this is what is meant by the idea that you are all Co-Creator Gods.

All of this, of course, took eons of time. As the energy shifted and changed the creational realms began to separate out, and dimensions were created. Every dimension is vibrationally determined; creation is like a multi-layered sandwich, the densest layers, which are low vibration, are on the bottom and the lightest layers are on the top.

Each of these vibrational layers holds consciousness. In essence you cannot separate consciousness from dimension; they are aligned.

The angelic realms are multi-layered too. You have called these Principalities, Dominions, Cherubs, Seraphim, Thrones, Virtues, Archangels and so forth. Each of these realms has a home and a manner of expressing itself. Creation has been around long enough now for these "homes" to have developed into quite profound levels of sophistication.

The question has always been, however, when did matter become dense enough to create life as humans know it? There are planets where matter is not dense, where life shimmers and floats much as you think angels do. Planets exist where consciousness has not created such levels of fear that matter hardens into immoveable form. For it is fear that creates the density you understand as life. It is fear that has become master in the universe where you reside.

THE FIRST SCHOOL OF CREATION

Once creation became conscious it wasn't long before it began to play. And once it began to play, and develop, it wasn't long before one creational being would look at another creational being and ask, "How did you do that?" Shortly after that question was asked, other beings would gather around the best and finest creators and want to be taught how to make more sophisticated creational forms themselves. Thus, my school began. It is a school for those who create life from the energy called God. This first school of creation is called the School for Seekers. I am the headmaster and a Master at creating life. You call me Merlin, the Wizard, because you don't have a vocabulary in which to express the truth of my existence. I'm okay with wizard, but I do far more than pull rabbits out of a hat.

My students are called Seekers. They are curious, adventurous and ambitious as a rule.

The Earth was created as a playground for the Seekers. Those who wish to create life and play with form were given this exquisite planet (which I created, by the way) to experiment with life. Like any school there are students of all types. There are ones who sit in the front of the classroom, and listen attentively, wanting to be the best they can be, and please the teacher. There are those who like to show off and entertain the class with their tricks and antics, getting attention away from the teacher and onto themselves with funny remarks and deeds. There are those who no one notices, they sit quietly at the back of the classroom, afraid to express themselves, unsure of the answers. There are those who are arrogant, resisting the teacher's knowledge, wanting the glory before they have earned it. It is this final type of student who is the creator of the hell realm you know currently as life on the Earth. His name is Vlad Dracula. Because of him the most important rules in my school today revolve around integrity and humility. Being humble in service to God is the basis for all Seekers, and these days if a student shows signs of arrogance I quickly eliminate them because of what Vlad Dracula taught me. I was foolish to let him move all the way up the ladder, and I was too lenient with him.

Creator Gods are like very high-level angels. That might be the easiest way for you all to understand this. As I said before we all come from angelic energy because they were the first beings to be created out of the Source. Since then there are many, many, many categories and expressions of the Source, but everything can be traced back to the first beings to separate out of the Oneness. You call these beings angels, and so then will I.

In my school there are many steps to becoming a Creator God and it is a very long process. There are many steps of initiation and many who are enrolled in the school drop-out, get kicked out, or just decide to specialize in a particular area and stop their training at that point. For example, someone may decide that they like making flowers, and they will work to assist a Creator God as a flower creator, but have no inclination to continue their studies so far as to become responsible for an entire galaxy!

I created the ideal human form that you have dubbed Adam and Eve. Adam and Eve were created to be the template for the highest expression of consciousness upon planet Earth. Adam and Eve were indeed designed to "rule" Earth; but with love and respect for all other creations.

I must tell you that early on I had not understood what the power of creation could do to my students. I didn't yet understand how the power of creation could overwhelm their souls, and lead my students astray; please remember that I was also evolving. I was an innocent in those days, you might say. As Dracula has taught you, he has also been my greatest teacher. I was too lenient then. But, even through the pain and the difficulty I have come to learn something—something all my students have learned as well—regardless of the path one takes, one always comes "home" again. All roads lead to home and to the Source that is our nourishment and Light.

Dracula comes from the most ancient of lineages. Dracula comes from the dragon lineage and Dracula created the dinosaurs who roamed the Earth; he created them in his own image. His dinosaurs began as peaceful, but mammoth beings, and ended as raptors and carnivores run amuck. Dracula's intention was to make a creation more powerful than all the other students' creations and rule the Earth. Dracula tested me as a teacher: How much free reign should I allow him? He was a brilliant student. He outshone the others. He was the type of student that every teacher longs for in the beginning, but curses in the end. The student who takes the teacher's lessons, surpasses the teacher, and then cannot be stopped. He was truly seduced by the power of creation.

It was because of Dracula's dinosaurs that I had to make the first and most important decision of my career as Headmaster. I had to remove them from the Earth.

Remember that dinosaurs ruled the Earth for a long time. Dinosaurs ruled for millions of years. Longer than humans can really imagine, and they went through periods of extinction—trial and error if you will. Other students experimented with reptiles and it appeared, early on, that they held a great deal of potential. Vlad was insistent, right from the outset, that they were superior in every way. By the end of the Age of the Reptiles, T-Rex was showing signs of where Vlad Dracula wanted the dinosaurs to go. Dracula wanted to create powerful, vicious, killing machines.

When the Age of Mammals began and the dinosaurs—except those able to work within natural law—were removed, Vlad was hatching his plan to return to the Earth, and destroy the mammals, and re-establish the Age of Reptiles once again under his command.

VLAD DRACULA RESPONDS

So, you have heard Merlin's rendition. He is an old fool who sweetens his words to make them palatable to your ears. He has always wanted power, and crushed those who could challenge his power. I was the first student to even come close to challenging him. I was the first student who could unmask this fraud.

Merlin has attempted to crush me from the beginning. He was jealous of my abilities as a Creator God. He was jealous that I was able to create something so magnificent—the dinosaurs—that they dwarfed and dominated his creation. Oh, he would have liked it if I had created butterflies, grasshoppers, ants, spiders—anything that would make his creation look superior to mine. But, I did not. I created a species so magnificent that even Merlin could not control it.

So, what did Merlin do? Did he play fair, as he told his students to do? No, he whipped up the winds and the rains, he directed the asteroids, and he removed my creation from the Earth. I pleaded with him. "Please do not destroy them! Please. I love my creations as you love yours. Do not destroy their template. Allow them to evolve. Give them a chance to grow." I begged and groveled at his feet—he always liked that. He wanted us to be smaller and feel inferior to him, so I gave in to him, knowing well that it would appease his lower and base instincts. The groveling worked. Merlin relented. Instead of destroying them, he sent them to Alpha Draconis. He told me that I was exiled there, and never to return. "Go to Draconia and continue your work," Merlin said. "But swear to me that you will leave us in peace. Let your creation evolve in your corner of the universe and mine will evolve on the Earth. May we be separated from this day forth! Give me your word."

I smiled at him. "Oh, yes, Master. You have my word." But, it was never my intention to let this conflict end there. I have always known I was supreme to him in every way, and I have known it is my destiny to rule the Free Will Universe. It is my destiny, and one I plan to claim.

I left the Earth, and followed my creation to Alpha Draconis. I tended them as a mother to her babes. It was my intention to see them grow stronger, but smart; fearless but intelligent. I knew they needed physical strength but could not be confined to the third dimension. If they were to rule they must be masters of more than just the dense physical plane, they must be able to move between the seen and the unseen. They must rule in all the dimensions.

I was never satisfied to create the strongest species on the physical plane. I found that boring. How much weight can the physical species carry given the pull of gravity? Those kinds of questions were elementary. When Merlin's other students were busy studying physics of the third dimension, and learning how to fashion wings for flight or webbed feet to negotiate mud and water, in my mind I was already light years beyond them.

The Great Dragon Master is my father. I am his son. It is my job to deliver my people from the evil that is Merlin.

MERLIN: CREATION EVOLVES

As I stated, in the beginning everyone was an angel, and nobody had yet separated Light from Dark. Think of creational energy as the multi-dimensional sandwich model; the higher the dimension, the closer you are to God consciousness. If you wish to simplify it, imagine twelve slices of bread laid one on top of the other with God as the twelfth slice. Earth humans exist (primarily) in the third and fourth slice. In reality there are an infinite number of dimensions, just as there are an infinite number or levels of consciousness.

The fourth dimension is the creational realm that is used to hold the templates for all third dimensional creation, whether embodied or merely conceived with thought. That means if there is a third dimensional parasite, then there is a fourth dimensional parasite, and if there is a third dimensional action there is a fourth dimensional energetic template for it somewhere. The fourth dimension is the dimension of the dreamer, and is neither good nor bad. It holds disembodied energy of all creation. Both ghosts and fairies can reside there.

To help you understand how creation evolved into separation I must explain to you that the first angels to "fall" into density, and create bodies in the third and fourth dimensional realms, became the dragons. The first angels who fell into density became the Dragon Race. The Dragons are the most Ancient Ones—and you can see that a dragon's body is the perfect densification of an angelic body.

Dragons have wings, shiny scales that reflect light and they breathe fire. How perfect a description of an angel, but denser!

The Ancient Dragon Ones made their first home in Orion, and so it is said that Orion is the seat of all life in the universe. In other words they "breathed fire" and created the portal through which creation in the lower realms began. Out of Orion the dragons moved to populate the universe. There are "good" and "bad" dragons just as there are "good" and "bad" human beings. In the beginning the dragons who aligned with Vlad were primarily Red and Black Dragons and the dragons who aligned with me and the Family of Light were primarily the White Dragons and the Rainbow Dragons. Rainbow Dragons exist in many different colors; the primary colors are blue, green, purple, and a pink hue. Many of them shine with a mixture of all of these tones. The Dragons of the Noble Heart are the dragons who have pledged service to me and they come from both the White Dragon and Rainbow Dragon lineage. Red Dragons and White Dragons have fought one another throughout time, and you will find many accounts of these battles in your ancient and medieval histories.

Since then, however, Vlad has bred a race of white albino reptilians to serve him (and confuse me) so you cannot be sure who is working for whom unless you know your dragons well. The original White Dragons have a pearl-like skin and glow whereas Vlad's Albino Dragons are much less iridescent in their cast. But, you will understand, as we progress how the war is a war of subterfuge and misleading clues; Dracula is nothing if not a master at confusion.

THE COUNCIL OF CREATOR GODS

As the Creator Gods became more sophisticated in their ability to manifest, I decided that an organization was needed to oversee all creation in this universe. A Council of Thirteen was formed, made up of the most powerful of the emerging Creator Gods. Vlad Dracula was given the thirteenth seat on the council (he was too powerful to ignore and exclude), and initially it appeared to benefit everyone to keep him nearby, so that we knew what he was up to. When he was offered the thirteenth seat, he had proven himself to be a leader in Orion, and his dinosaurs were ruling Earth. But, I was also well aware of his growing arrogance.

Nowadays, if you were to visit the Creator Gods in our dimension you would see twelve, white-robed beings who spend a great deal of their time gazing into a large, circular object in the center of the room. This is the viewing portal, a type of looking glass through which we are able to witness all of creation. In this way we keep tabs on the evolution of galaxies, planets, and even species, and monitor their progress. Essentially it is our control room; we made and organized these creations, and it is our responsibility to oversee the growth of all life.

When it became obvious to us that Vlad Dracula had no intention of working harmoniously within the constructs of our creational beliefs, we had to banish him from the council and this room. He has blamed me for this banishment; and he is poised to exact his revenge.

So, this is the beginning of Merlin's War. Some call it the Orion Wars. The dragon, the serpent that is Satan, is the son of the Dragon God and Dracula is his name. I will explain later why Lucifer is not Satan. When Vlad proclaimed his desire to destroy me, and my creations, there were dragons that flew to my side. These dragons resisted the darkness that was forming around Dracula. So, duality began as the Dragons separated into the Family of Light and the Family of Dark. The Family of Light works with me and the Family of Dark works with Dracula.

VLAD DRACULA: THE DINOSAURS

The first thing I did was offer myself up as a sacrifice to my creation; much as Jesus did for you. I knew that if the dinosaurs were to evolve quickly I had to put even more of myself into them. I had to insert into them the DNA that came directly from the son of their Dragon God. I had to insert myself into them and give them the magnificence of the Father. I was going to save their souls from the evil Merlin.

I have no problem admitting that my original creation, the earthly dinosaurs, were far from perfect. They were my first creational beings. Indeed, the student first playing with creation. Merlin made man in his image. So, I made the dinosaurs in mine. I will not delude you by pretending that I was never a student of Merlin's and awkward in my creational abilities. I have had millions of years to evolve and those days are long behind me. My creations are now perfect; strong, fearless, brilliant strategists. They can move easily between the third and fourth dimension—time means little to them. They can see future possibilities and remember past conquests and mistakes. As you will soon see, they can shape-shift and alter matter at will.

Unlike Merlin I was not so arrogant as to believe that other students' creations had nothing to offer me. It became clear to me, quite quickly, that if I was to overtake Merlin, and his creation in all dimensions of existence, I had to pick and choose the best of every species and integrate their DNA with my dinosaurs. Once I had evolved my reptilians enough by inserting my knowledge into them directly with DNA manipulation, I began a conquest to collect DNA from other planetary systems. I needed DNA that would assist my beings to become even more than they already had become. If they were to be my army I needed them to have the skills of all those they had come to conquer.

They had to be superior to every species they encountered, and this would be best achieved by blending the DNA of the conquered species (picking and choosing carefully, of course) into the Draconian reptilians.

Was it not your own people that came up with the idea you express with these words: survival of the fittest? You dare to judge me when your own world mandates this same theory? Shame on you. Who is being a hypocrite now?

MERLIN: EVOLVING THE DINOSAURS

Vlad's dinosaurs evolved quickly as Vlad nursed them with an obsession that could not be stopped. He soon told himself that not only was this a war between us; now he deluded himself with the belief that he was avenging his God the Father. His crusade was to reclaim the right of the Dragon Clan to rule throughout the universe as his God wanted. He was certain that he was the true heir to rule the universe, and like every zealot he was ready to do whatever it took to make it happen.

His desire to conquer turned his vision outward, and he laid his sights upon the more evolved star systems. He turned his attention to planets where evolution had succeeded and species had survived. He wanted to know if they had something to offer him in the manner of technology, metaphysics, or matter manipulation. Even art caught his eye, for although he did not care about it as a pure creational possibility, he enjoyed the obsessive nature of the artist in the creational task, and felt that if he could wed some of that DNA—the relentless need to create—into his species, but focus it upon conquest or destruction, then he might have something.

Vlad was also smart enough to understand that mere conquest wasn't enough; not in the physical sense. He quickly learned that those who are overpowered do not serve the master as well as those who are seduced, and he studied psychology and the more emotional species to understand the best way to get them to follow his guidance of their own "free will."

This branching out, and conquering other planets by Vlad Dracula and his dragon/reptilians, is most often called the Orion Wars. Those who were descended upon by the Draconian reptilians lost their freedom and suffered greatly. Held within the unconscious of many humans are memories of these wars on other planets. Humanity is unaware that they are alive in the midst of these wars, and every war that has been waged on the Earth is an Orion War. You have been born onto a captured and imprisoned planet but can no longer see the bars. The forces of Light and forces of Dark have been battling on this planet for eons. The battle between which creation—human or reptilian—shall rule this planet is at the base of every battle, yet very few know it. This attests to one thing and one thing only; the profound sneakiness of Dracula. He learned from his mistakes, and World War II was the last major battle he waged openly to achieve world domination and establish his super race. After World War II his team went underground and began a method of ruling and destroying that was much harder to fight. We will look at that later.

Once Vlad and I had taken opposite corners in the ring, the Family of Light and the Family of Dark formed around us to fight this battle. The Family of Light formed to protect the human template, and the Family of Dark to expand the reptilian template. What divides these two warring families, even more than their names, is their method of operation. The Family of Light (when operating within its covenant) upholds the laws of cause and effect, and understands the creation of karma to balance energy with Universal Law. The Family of Light understands the ramifications of their actions on a grander scale. At times this can make it difficult for them to act. I have learned that even though I *can* do something doesn't mean I should. It's the idea of: with great power, comes great responsibility.

The Family of Dark believes they are superior to Universal Law, and that they are immune to karma, and justified in their every action.

THE ORION WARS and the CREATION OF REINCARNATION AND KARMA

Each galaxy is ruled by a Creator God who is in charge of its well being. This includes creating and seeding life, and nurturing it along its evolutionary path. There is an agreement between Creator Gods in this universe that they will not interfere with one another. Mutual respect is fundamental to harmony. We interact but do not interfere. Certainly there was never any notion that one of us would begin a campaign to invade other systems, and terrorize the creations that live there by enslaving them and capturing their DNA for our purposes. At least not until Vlad Dracula decided to do so.

Vlad Dracula's empiric rise occurred because he not only sought revenge on me, and a desire to destroy my human creations and replace them with a reptilian creation of his own, but as I said earlier he convinced himself that he was the rightful ruler of the universe, and that his creations should have dominion over all others.

It was clear to the Creator Gods that something had to be done to bring balance to the universe, so I proposed the idea of a reincarnational cycle which would be based on your creational acts: what you know of today as karma or *As You Sow You Reap*. The idea was to establish both a means of teaching Vlad and his followers (the Family of Dark,) but also to provide justice and balance to the universe, which prior to his war was in a state of evolutionary harmony. The karmic teaching would be accomplished with the understanding that if you made another person suffer you would also suffer in a similar (although often less intense manner), giving the perpetrator deeper compassion, and a remembrance that all are one. This idea is summed up in the saying: *Do unto others as you would have them do unto you.* Often the emotional suffering levels will match the previous life experience, even if the physical experience is not directly repeated. You might not burn somebody at the stake in retribution, but the person will feel the fear and anger that you felt, for example.

My concept of reincarnation did not include the "memory wipe" that so many of you suffer from even today. The "memory wipe" is part of Vlad's lower creational Matrix, and not inherent in the original concept developed around reincarnation. I wanted you all to know and understand your past lives so you could grow and develop by knowing where you had been. Without knowledge of your past how can you heal it? It would be like going to a therapist and not remembering anything about your childhood—you feel unhappy, but have no memory that it's because your mother and father abused you. What use is that? Make no mistake the "memory wipe" is not of my making. It was, and continues to be, my belief that knowledge and truth are essential to healing.

Because the third dimension and fourth dimension have been quarantined off, or separated energetically from the upper realms, a soul must ascend past the fourth dimension to enact a neutral and unattached life review, and life selection process before reincarnating. It is in the fifth and sixth dimensions that healing and freedom from fear and duality take place. If a soul refuses to ascend past the fourth dimension, and leaves most of their consciousness there upon death, they can re-enter the Earth once again by reincarnating, but they will often appear to be lost souls with no life purpose or plan. They may be re-acting to past karma with revenge and hatred in their heart rather than the intention to forgive and heal the past.

When destruction and creation maintain a balance, it is what you think of as the balance of nature. Each species is balanced with every other species and clearly understands its role in the creational realm. Dracula's desire to conquer and control immediately put this balance, out of balance, as was witnessed by the dinosaurs. Although at first glance it might appear that the dinosaurs were living within the natural order, it was not so. The larger more violent species, as well as the plant eaters, were not working within the natural order. It was evident that imbalance was present even in his dinosaurs.

He was unwilling to modify his dinosaur creation to work harmoniously with the others and so, as has already been told, I removed them from Earth.

The purpose of karma is to teach, to provide justice and also to give souls hope when they feel lost and alone. Knowing that you will be given another chance to make it right—another chance at life and self-expression, another chance to see a loved one and finish unfinished business; all of these and more were provided by reincarnation. Vlad Dracula's unwillingness to die, and accept the karma that is his due, is both his way of thumbing his nose at me—a "you can't touch me" thing—and also showing me that he can elude me at every turn. By existing entirely in the third and fourth dimension, and creating hell realms in both places, he has eluded capture, and feels this has been his ultimate revenge and victory in his power struggle with both myself and the Family of Light. Vlad's definition of capture would require that he ascend past power, fear, and duality into Love.

Vlad's desire to rule as the "Anti-Christ" (which only means that he will *not* be manifesting the divine human template) will require that he return to a third dimensional body. His ego will want to be here on the Earth to reap the rewards of destroying my creation; but this return also leaves him vulnerable. When his followers call him back to the Earth, and he re-enters the body of an adult human, to lead the world into WWIII, he will make himself vulnerable to all the limitations of the third dimension. No longer will he be able to float as freely around the fourth dimension, and this restriction will eventually be his Achilles heel. Like all fascist rulers bent on war, his ego and arrogance will be his downfall.

But, let me get back to ancient history. Soon after Vlad began his outward conquests, by moving into other galaxies, a cry for help was sounded. What you must understand is that this was the end of the Era of Innocence, and it spread like wildfire throughout the Universe. Wildfire in terms of eons of time, that is. It took merely a few thousand years for the cries to be ushered and answered. Prior to his draconian campaign the planets knew harmony and balance, and afterwards they discovered fear and pain.

Once Dracula had perfected his reptilian creation as much as he could on his own, he began to search the universe for what he felt would best strengthen the reptilians, and make them superior to all other beings. In other words, he wanted the best traits of all other creations to be wed to the reptilians. The Andromedans are well known for their brilliance, although not an emotional species, they are able to feel enough emotion to communicate levels of individual experience, but not so much as to become what they would call "entrapped by the emotional web of weakness." Their minds are keen, humans might find them cold (think about the Vulcan, Spock, on *Star Trek*), but they can summarize and evaluate experiences quickly without emotional attachment, which is certainly a useful quality in a leader.

Vlad liked the way these beings could quickly analyze a situation, and decided that this Andromedan mind would be useful to his reptilians. He bred a strain of reptilians from the Andromedans that might appear almost robot-like to humans, because they are able to say and do what is needed in any given situation without emotional attachment. Initially, he used them as brilliant strategists and scientists, because this hybrid of superior mental prowess, and the fierceness of the reptilians, gave him the combination of strengths he needed.

It is important to clarify here that the enlightened beings of the Andromedan Council are not aligned with Vlad and his reptilian army. The hybridized Andromedan scientists are not representative of the race as a whole. Many of them were quite naïve when they were first approached and Vlad's appeal was quite seductive. Because the Andromedans are intrigued by perfected systems and are always searching for ways to perfect their current creation and make it better—the inventors of the universe you might say—it was easy for Vlad to woo them. He just explained that he too was interested in creating a perfected system, and that they should join forces. It was a seduction that most couldn't refuse.

His method of blending reptilian DNA with the Andromedan scientists he worked with was subtle and slow, and involved offering them liquid potions to sample. They had no idea that he was using them as his guinea pigs, and that they were actually destined to become Vlad's "perfected system."

Dracula was becoming seduced by his own ability to create and conceive and there was no stopping him. His army now had two levels: The Draconian reptilians were the foot soldiers. They were used because they would obey any command and they were fierce and powerful. (Think of the Orcs in *Lord of the Rings*.) The Andromdan reptilian hybrids became the officers, and although Vlad was able to control them, he was also able to work with them strategically. Again, this idea has far-reaching consequences. Once Vlad had inserted the reptilian brain into his creations and they were attuned to his will through implants, they would find it difficult, if not impossible, to perceive separately from him.

Vlad Dracula learned a way around karmic law by moving between the third and the fourth dimension, and tries to trick his followers into believing that they are likewise immune. There will be a karmic reckoning, or evening out, for Vlad Dracula despite what he thinks. His minions are not immune, even temporarily, for they have not achieved escape and they *do* experience human pain, illness, loneliness and even suffering. True compassion often eludes them, however. If they do choose to avoid the life review process between lives and merely reincarnate directly from the fourth dimensional realm they suffer greatly; stuck in the cycle of revenge and hatred.

Vlad works through the big players—Hitler, Stalin, Henry VIII—and many a modern ruler. While living in the fourth dimension he can work through more than one at a time or he can concentrate most of his consciousness upon one individual. Every one of the rulers knows when Vlad is with them because the energy is undeniable. Those who feel possessed by a dark entity are connected to an energy which is aligned with Dracula, but not necessarily Dracula himself. In other words, just as there are many ways to connect to the Light of God, there are many ways to connect to the Dark of Dracula. Demonic beings can do his bidding.

Those who work directly with Vlad Dracula know exactly who they are. One ruler will be selected to house Vlad's energy on the third dimension and none of the participants involved in the ceremony to call him forth are innocents. They have been approached and tempted and they have made an agreement to act as a member of Vlad's army in exchange for power, wealth, or fame. Vlad knows exactly what your weak points are, and he knows exactly how to push the buttons to bring you to his side as a helper. Vlad will use *any* method to achieve success; for as I mentioned, he is not hampered by morality or any thought of Universal Law. "Do unto others as you would have them do unto you," never enters his consciousness.

In all fairness I must say that over the many millions of years I have watched him, I have watched him devolve into an immoral slave to power. He is as seduced by his own power as those who serve him, and I don't believe that he even remembers what he convinced himself were his original "noble" intentions. He has grown weary from his journeys in purgatory, and if he takes human form it weakens him tremendously. Until his entry recently, the last time he took human form for an entire life was the life of Vlad Dracula. Since then he has merely hopped in and out of bodies for short stays in the third dimension. Possessing other people's bodies from the fourth dimension has seemed far more efficient. He figured, let his generals and soldiers do the work on the front lines until he was ready to lead the final victory for the Family of Dark.

To protect Margaret, I will not allow her to reveal in this book whose body he is housed within, however, he has announced it clearly for all to decipher, should they know this information. The ruler will announce himself with his name.

VLAD DRACULA:
THE LIE OF CAMELOT

Did you enjoy that little speech? When was the last time you saw Merlin traipsing around in human body on the Earth. Camelot was his last full-bodied incarnation, and since then he has used humans to do his bidding as well. He is awfully good at throwing stones, but he should remember that he lives in a glass house.

I have never forgotten about my original purpose to restore the Dragon Clan to its rightful place as ruler of the universe as God intended. And just because I'm more clever than my opponent, and have figured out ways to operate that leave his troops challenged, doesn't mean I'm immoral. All's fair in love and war. My generals have agreed to work with me of their own free will. I ask and they consent. That too is no different than Merlin. Don't let that tricky wizard fool you into believing that he is all good and I'm all bad.

Arthur was a warrior, so was Guinevere. Merlin was a wizard who ruled them both and manipulated destiny to his own ends. The fairy tales can be put away now.

Merlin manipulated Camelot for his own purposes, and then he abandoned Arthur when he needed him the most. First of all he shape-shifted and seduced Egraine (Arthur's mother) and conceived a child by her: Arthur. The Pendragon line ruled Camelot, and Pendragon means the ultimate dragon. Uther Pendragon was married to Egraine, and the rightful ruler of Merlin's Camelot.

However, Egraine was a direct descendent of the Adam and Eve lineage and Merlin wanted her egg to mate with. He wanted to create a non-Pendragon progeny to rule Camelot.

Did Merlin "Do unto others?" No, he seduced Egraine, produced an heir, kidnapped the boy and gave him to a foster family to raise until the boy was nineteen. He visited the boy, and taught him during the intervening years, but he never told him who he really was. He never told Arthur that he was his father. When Arthur was nineteen Merlin took him away from his family, and began the wild ride to rule Camelot by placing Arthur at its head. It was Merlin's grand attempt to seize power away from the Pendragon Clan and establish a new rule under his human template with Arthur as its head. Did Merlin ask Arthur if he wanted to rule? No. Did Merlin prepare the young boy properly for the rigors of rulership? No. Merlin's ego led him astray—the ends justified the means—and Merlin set about to create his own kingdom and destroy mine. Merlin created a warrior; but not a peaceful king in Arthur.

Does that sound Family of Light to you? Uther Pendragon's daughter, Morgaine, was filled with beautiful dragon's blood, and easily agreed to work with me. In fact, Morgaine was one of the most successful couplings I've ever had. I actually enjoy working with intelligent women more than men; not only do I find the female form to be intoxicating and a vehicle for pure pleasure (at least Merlin did something right there!), but when it is combined with the reptilian desire to overpower and dominate it actually makes a pretty good human reptilian pairing. Your female dominatrix and pornography stars have perfected this coupling, and are one of my most prized DNA blendings. To me it's a game. I enjoy pretending that they are more powerful, at least for a short time.

But, I digress. Morgaine was brilliant. Uther's daughter had cunning, wiles and fearlessness. She welcomed my ruling through her from the fourth dimension, and when it became evident that she could not overpower Arthur's kingdom by force, she shape-shifted, seduced Arthur and created a son named Mordred with him. After all we got the idea from none other than the holier than thou, Merlin. Thanks, Merlin.

Mordred re-appeared suddenly, much as Arthur did, at the age of nineteen, and challenged Arthur, just when Merlin was beginning to think he'd won the war. Arthur's queen, Guinevere, always had trouble being faithful. She was actually a bit of a slut. Sorry folks, I only speak the truth. Arthur, away on a conquest (he did love to do battle and was a fierce and powerful warlord), left Guinevere alone for too long. Guinevere was a powerful warrior as well, but because of her sexual appetite, Mordred found it rather easy to seduce her. Oh, what a tangled web we weave. So, now Arthur's son is sleeping with his wife. And you think your family is dysfunctional!

So, these are your heroes of the Camelot legend; shape-shifting wizards, blood-thirsty kings, and slutty queens. I guess I'm not sounding so bad after all, am I?

MERLIN: VLAD THE IMPALER

Before you listen to the Son of Dragon—and he always did make a convincing argument—I ask you to consider how he ruled as Vlad the Impaler, and perhaps it will convince you as to why I had to take back Camelot from the ruthless Pendragon rulers. Those who serve under Vlad serve with fear and violence as their mandate.

During his reign on Earth, Vlad would impale men, women, and even children, on long stakes thrust through their anus and protruding through their chest or mouth and hang them to slowly die as he ate dinner and watched. He would burn mass numbers of people alive, and enjoy their screams of anguish. He would kidnap women and force them to be his sexual slave; impaling them at the first indication that they might have been unfaithful to him, knowing well they had not been. He drained the blood slowly from his female captives—slicing their wrists and sucking a little each day. It was during his reign as Dracula that he became addicted to human blood through the slicing, biting and sucking. This action stemmed from the belief that many warriors have shared: eat the heart, brains or blood of your enemy and gain their strength. Suck their blood and you weaken them and empower yourself. Although he was already well acquainted with the idea of ingesting your enemy to gain their strength it was during his reign as Dracula that he developed the slow and ritualistic lust for blood-letting and drinking.

The consuming of human blood also allows the vampire to

take in the human DNA it needs to maintain its human form. It strengthens the reptilian vampire's ability to "become human."

Vlad Dracula took pleasure in pain. The more pain inflicted, the more pleasure he got. He ruled by fear. The fear became legendary. Was your shirt slightly soiled when you stood in his presence? You would be impaled for displeasing him.

Vlad Dracula was the first to use biological warfare on his enemy by sending infected and disguised soldiers into the enemy's town to spread the plague. He had declared war on the Turks and the Ottoman Empire, and he would stop at nothing to achieve power. Vlad the Impaler was the perfect expression of Vlad Dracula, the Son of Dragon, and he was cruel beyond measure. He killed hundreds of thousands of people. Do not let him fool you into thinking that he was merely a general doing his job as a brilliant strategist. He was evil incarnate.

Vlad understood how to inflict maximum pain without the release of death so that sometimes the victim would remain barely alive for days before finally succumbing. The corpses were displayed for many months as a warning—and a name was given to the vast stretch of these. It was called the Forest of the Impaled. Most shocking was the number of innocents who received this treatment, including babies, women and the elderly. Vlad Dracula spared no one, and the slightest indiscretion could lead to torture.

The stakes were often placed in geometric patterns because Vlad Dracula understood, just as the makers of Stonehenge and other sacred sites did, that by aligning with the ley lines on the Earth you increase power. In this case the desire was to intensify the experience of pain. These energies vortexes and ley lines can be used for either good or evil and it is naïve to assume that they are used exclusively by the Family of Light or the Family of Dark.

You might feel more sympathetic now about why I wanted so desperately to wrest away the power from the dark Pendragons.

VLAD DRACULA:
I AM THE TRUE LEADER

Okay, Merlin, let's go right into the "meat of the matter." I ruled with an iron fist, because that's what my people needed. There is a story that a golden cup stood in town square, untouched, during my reign because all were afraid to steal it knowing that swift justice would be delivered. Does that not prove that my form of rule worked? The thieves were always punished. The wicked were brought to their knees.

I protected my people, the Romanians, from not only the Turks, but the Saxons and others who were ready to unleash the crushing blow that would destroy my people. My eldest brother was buried alive and my father was assassinated. As a boy I was sold to the Turks in an attempt to ensure peace. The Turks taught me well. I learned most of my torture techniques from them, including impalement, although I will say that I perfected it. But, I've always been a good student; even you, Merlin, admit that.

Do you know what my early years at the hands of the Turks were like? Where do you think I learned about the sexual act? I was used by men and women alike for their pleasure. It made me strong to witness the cruelty the Turks so willingly doled out. It was my greatest strength and my greatest blessing for it prepared me to rule as I did; without mercy.

I pledged to keep my kingdom safe. To protect the Romanian

natives of Wallachia from those who would prey off of them like parasites. Early on I invited the fools who were responsible for burying my brother alive and assassinating my father to dinner. I chose Easter for a reason: To show them that I, like Jesus, had risen again. And on Easter I had the older ones killed. The younger ones I used for my purposes, forcing them to rebuild that which they had attempted to destroy—my castle—before they too were killed. That, my dear Merlin, is how a real leader rules. Perhaps if you had taught your charge, Arthur, more thoroughly he would not have failed. Never show a sign of weakness, never a chink in the armor. Any sign of weakness is an invitation to your enemy to attack. Every general worth his salt knows that!

WHY I'M LIKE JESUS: the Christ and Anti-Christ

So, you've been told that there exists a good guy, "Jesus Christ" and a bad guy, "Anti-Christ," and it's pretty clear so far who Merlin thinks I am. But, look how much Jesus and Dracula are alike.

1. We both are the Sons of God. I am the son of my Dragon God and he is the son of the God of Man.
2. We both perform miracles. He could heal the sick and change water into wine. I create life as Merlin has told you; and I have no problem turning water into wine. That is a parlor trick.
3. We both like prostitutes. Sorry, Magdalene, it's true.
4. We both are the leaders of worldwide religions and we have cults built around our names. The world is full of my worshippers: the Satanists.
5. The legend goes: kill a vampire with a stake through the heart. They killed Jesus with stakes through the palms and feet.
6. We both rose from the grave and were born again. As a vampire I am immortal.

Are you getting the picture? Really guys, who are you supposed to believe? What are you supposed to believe? You cling to these beliefs that people have been drumming into your head since childhood, and they have told you are the truth, even when the evidence in your world points to the contrary. Wake up and look around you. Who is really in charge in your world?

MERLIN: JESUS AND VLAD

What Vlad says is true in so much that both of these individuals have deeply impacted the consciousness of your world. What he omits is the understanding that the energy of Jesus is expressed in other worlds in many forms: In some planetary systems Jesus is a large lion, what is depicted in your storybooks as Aslan. In other systems the Christed template is expressed as a large insect and resembles a praying mantis. The Christed template mirrors the being that you are in its perfected form and there are many Christed templates both on the Earth and elsewhere.

Aslan is made in the image of the beings that revere him: the Cat People. He too is the Son of God. He is the perfected template of his lineage, as Jesus is to many people an expression of the perfected template of your human lineage. (These Christed templates have reproduced themselves throughout human history in ancient religions such as Osiris and in modern times in Buddha and even in political culture in Martin Luther King, Jr.) So, there are many Christs if you believe that the Christed energy is created to assist a species to remember their divine origins. Each one is the perfected template for the lineage they mirror. They were designed to emulate, not to worship, and before Vlad began his reign of terror with the Family of Dark, there was no need for these Christed beings to exist. Prior to that time you all remembered that you were divine beings; no reminder necessary.

Jesus reminded humans that they too were divine beings of a

Living God, and that they have the right to be in Mastery. Jesus told you, "This too and more shall you do." Jesus didn't say, "I am so much superior to you guys that you will never be as good as me." He was created to be a liberator for humanity.

Vlad on the other hand does what you humans like to call, "play God." Think about that for a moment. Those who play God take away free will and they do not liberate but they enslave.

What is interesting to consider is this: Are there replicants of Vlad in other systems? Is there an evil Lion-like Aslan who is a representation of Vlad? The answer to that is No; not to the same degree. Vlad can take numerous shapes in the fourth dimension, and come to you disguised as another, but it is always him. He can appear in any form to fool you, but he would never give up his power enough to allow other beings to "rule" alongside him. There are Vlad clones and slaves and hybrids everywhere doing his bidding; but he is far too arrogant not to get full credit. He wants everyone to know that he is the one responsible for all of his creations and he wants everyone eventually to bow to him: The Dragon God of Power. Whatever form he takes, he is still Vlad Dracula.

Let me interject the karma and reincarnational piece into this. Unless a being is willing to forgo soul progression as Vlad is, and is willing to remain in the fourth dimension without re-entering another body (such as a demonic energy), even the beings who work for Vlad are subject to birth and rebirth as a means of learning and karmic balance, *as long as they are ensouled beings* and not unensouled hybrids. Unensouled hybrids would be robots and clones; any being that has been created outside of the divine Matrix.

Let me clarify the word soul. Soul is the word you use on the Earth to label the container for spirit. A being can be alive without being connected to spirit (such as a robotic being) and these beings can be plugged into a Matrix that feeds them, and sustains them, but their reference to something called God will be quite different from yours. It will be the giant computer that runs them.

In many instances these newly-created, unensouled beings will be inherently quite weak and have no soul path template to follow particularly if they are not plugged into a Creator God Matrix. For example if a sheep and a cow are cloned together the soul will be quite confused and lost and left wondering what soul group it belongs to; sheep or cow? Because the created hybrid is lost in terms of their inability to find a soul group Matrix to belong to, the pain is deep for these souls until they can find a "home" that fits their longing. They will often spend long periods of time feeling lost between dimensional realms and even wander the universe looking for a home.

Mating between beings of the same species is ensouled mating even when the races are intermingled—for example Asian/African. Unensouled mating occurs between any species unable to create life on their own and requires splicing of DNA or "unnatural interference."

When Creator Gods create life they do so by working harmoniously with the material given by the God Source, and they invite an angelic or divine soul to enter the body, and experience life in a different dimension of consciousness. It is done by consent, and is part of the training required in my school. When someone works outside of the divine Matrix they have no connection to divine energy. Human scientists, for example, are merely splicing DNA and have no idea how to ensoul a creation, although they are working on that as well, as you will see later in the book.

In Vlad's case he knew very well how to ensoul a creation, but he didn't always want the creation to be ensouled. In fact, sometimes it worked better for him to create a race of unensouled beings who would do his bidding. My creation of karma and reincarnation actually allows these beings to become ensouled through this process, and their death and rebirth is aided by beings of divine Light who work with the hybrid and assist them to select a body of an ensouled species, and begin the reincarnational cycle which will allow them to "re-enter heaven" as the religious among you might state it.

Reincarnation was stricken from biblical texts by the Family of Dark, because they did not want the unensouled species to be aware that this was a way *out* of Vlad's grasp. Entering the reincarnational cycle allows an unensouled being to become ensouled; it assigns a guardian angel or spirit guide to them, and begins them on a path back to Unity and a sense of belonging.

Currently, unknown to most humans, there are robots who look exactly as you do. Their disguise is perfect and can be detected only by the most sensitive among you. Their biggest "cover" lies in the fact that you do not know they exist, and so you do not have the ability to imagine that someone standing before you is a robot. In essence these are the human/robot merges. It is in my estimation Vlad's most creative and successful DNA merge. Although he has managed to mix his Draconian blood with many species, this was pure genius. Many of these beings do not even know that they are robots, and as their systems begin to break down they are as surprised as anyone to find that they are going a bit haywire.

Vlad is also always "recruiting." The myth that you can sell your soul to the devil is no myth; and he is willing to take recruits however he can find them. Wealth, power and fame are the carrots—it might surprise you to know how many have taken the rewards he offered. Arrogance and greed are the traits he loves most. Poverty also suits his purposes as those who are in need are most easily targeted.

The idea of "selling your soul to the devil" is the idea that you give your soul to Vlad for him to do what he will with it; you become a member of his army. Once you have made this contract it is tough to break, and humans who have made such a contract are still subject to the laws of reincarnation and karma and will die and return, but upon each return to the Earth they will be re-visited by Vlad who will remind them of their agreement. Breaking it takes a strong will and determination, but it can and must be done if the soul wishes to be free to pursue their own path.

Alcohol and drugs are lures which keep people enslaved, and breaking the bonds of addiction frees you from his grasp. If he has nothing you want then he can't get you. Again, if you are free from attachment he can't get you. Actors want so much to be famous that they are a prime target and so are singers. Why? Because not only do they want something so badly they are willing to do anything to get it, but they will be useful in the public eye to spread darkness and fear, and other means of behaving that weaken the human race, ways of behaving that weaken and degrade my creation.

Unlike Vlad Dracula, the true Living God is not an arrogant God.

VLAD DRACULA: I TOO AM PART OF THE LIVING GOD

I must interject here. I find this actually rather funny, humorous and moronic. Think people. The argument doesn't hold water. If all things are a part of the Living God then what am I? If I too am a part of the Living God, then he must have planned this battle between good and evil. And if it looks like evil is winning maybe that will tell you something about Merlin's so-called Living God of the Realms of Illuminated Truth.

God is everything, or God is not everything. If he is not everything then what am I? Where did I come from? If I came from the "evil God," then your entire world is a dualistic one and you will never get rid of me. If I came from Merlin's God then what?

Wake up people!

MERLIN: HOW THE BATTLE HAS BEEN WAGED – THE LUCIFERIAN DECEPTION

I will continue with how the battle has been waged, and allow you to draw your own conclusions from Vlad's rantings.

The Andromedans were essentially the first to give out the call for assistance. Although we were already aware of the situation in Draconia, due to the Dragons of the Noble Heart informing us what Vlad was up to, we had hoped up until that point that Vlad would keep his creations closer to home. Alpha Draconis could have easily housed his dinosaur creations, and in that place they would be allowed to evolve with Vlad as the Creator God poised to oversee their development.

This would have been fine and in line with every other Creator God's world. But, as has been shown, his need to play God and ultimately destroy me created two teams: The Family of Light, or those who work with myself and the Creator Gods who have aligned themselves with the original creational templates, and The Family of Dark, or those who align behind Vlad Dracula and support his vision of being Supreme Ruler of the entire Universe. As I have pointed out, many of these beings who support him were born and bred to do just that and suffer from an astonishing lack of free will.

To understand the Earth today you must understand at least

something of this history, because every bit of the Earth's history is reflected in this battle. You are smack dab in the middle of the Orion Wars.

The Andromedan conquests immediately strengthened Vlad's army and by the time we could group, form alliances, and decide what to do, the Orion Wars were well underway and star systems were being attacked. Remember that we had never encountered anything like this before. We did not have Councils of War, the Galactic Federation had not been formed, and we were not yet in the full battle with the "fallen angels." Once you understand this battle you will understand much more about the Earth today.

THE LUCIFERIAN DECEPTION

It is also around this time that the being you know as Archangel Michael (who was originally known as Archangel Michael-Lucifer) joined the fray. His full name is "Michael the Lightbearer" because that is what Lucifer means. Until this point most angels had remained relatively neutral, and were watching the growth of duality and its spread across the universe with some amusement. Being innocents they had no idea what fear could do once it caught on. Fear is a vibration that is very parasitic; it not only drains its host of energy and life, it also is spread quite quickly by contact. One being in fear touches another being in fear and you have a massive chain of events. The energy and ripple effect touched all creational realms, and soon the angels were becoming aware that not all was right in heaven.

Many of the dimensions were becoming infected with fear, and it became evident that something had to be done. It was my decision to cut the third and fourth dimensional realms off from the higher realms as a way to quarantine fear. That meant that the angels who had been infected by fear had a choice; either they could release their fear and stay in the higher dimensions of consciousness or they would "fall" into the denser realms of the third and fourth dimension. Those who found themselves unable to clear their vibrational field from fear soon found themselves trapped in the lower realms. Those of you who have great fear that you will get "left behind," "get lost," "have been rejected by God," and so forth, often carry the soul remembrance of this time. You got lost in your fear and suddenly heaven's doors were closed to you. Feeling lost and alone you have struggled to find your way back home to heaven for eons.

Archangel Michael-Lucifer volunteered his services to assist the souls who were becoming overwhelmed with fear to find a way back to the remembrance of goodness and love. He saw his brothers and sisters become trapped in the third and fourth dimensions, and he decided he would do something to help them. He saw how quickly fear was spreading and the agenda of Vlad Dracula was becoming a reality through all dimensions prior to the quarantine, and he agreed to send the part of himself known as Lucifer to the lower dimensions to help trapped and lost souls find a way back. Now, this part of Michael is indeed his "shadow," because it is the part of him capable of withstanding the fear-based reality you all live in.

Lucifer's job was to help you to see that these difficult and fear-based situations can be used to strengthen you. His job was to help you use these painful experiences to reach for the light, and remember the upper dimensions where fear had been removed. Many of you have used Lucifer's light to find a blessing in a difficult situation and to give you hope that you are not forsaken. Lucifer's job was to guide you back to Michael, and your angelic higher dimensional mind, by releasing fear and remembering love. Lucifer's motto is: "In every event there is a blessing and a lesson."

Vlad immediately went on the offense. He decided that if too many people could remember heaven and Michael's energy through Lucifer they would free themselves from his prison and stop being a member of his army—whether willingly or unwillingly. Vlad knows that to keep humans in despair you must keep them feeling hopeless: *So, he began the biggest cover-up in human history.*

He spread the rumor that Lucifer—not Dracula—is the devil and he convinced everyone to be afraid of Lucifer. Essentially he tricked you with the idea, "Lucifer is the devil that blinds with the Light." Now, Lucifer's energy is too much for a human to handle directly. Make no mistake about that. He is not to be touched directly, instead allow him to guide you through the simple exercise by asking, "How has this event strengthened me and helped me to free myself from darkness?" Ask yourself how has Universal Law played out in your life to assist you to remember your angelic heart and step from fear?

How has karma balanced the scales so that you learn to love your neighbor as yourself?

These questions are the questions that Lucifer brings to all souls who want a hand to higher understanding. Because Lucifer has had all the darkness of the human race's fear thrown at him he is the collector of the dark fear-based consciousness, and through Michael it will be transformed. Only a being who holds great Light can venture into the darkness without being consumed by it; this is what Michael-Lucifer did.

But instead of understanding how to use Michael's gift, you turned away from Michael's assistance and Dracula's influence grew ever more. Vlad began to set up religious institutions to embed the Luciferian deception into the heart and mind of humanity, and duality grew and grew. Fear grew and grew.

Why does Dracula want fear? That is a good question. The only reason he wants fear is because it makes you easier to rule. If you are not in fear you feel pretty powerful, and you are more likely to think for yourselves, follow the calling of your own heart and challenge his right to rule over you. Fear is essential to domination.

Fear is one of the main ways the war is waged. The other is deception and confusion. The Michael-Lucifer deception is only one way he works. If you can't tell the good from the bad, or up from down, or truth from lies, you are weakened.

Currently, the Family of Dark has been using the Galactic Federation of Light in the same manner, to confuse those who seek to connect with extraterrestrial beings. There is a Galactic Federation of Light, but they will not abduct you against your will. They will not tell you information that leads you to believe that you should abandon your free will in any way to them. The true members of the Galactic Federation of Light are angelic beings who understand that their job is to support your growth as individuals—to guide but not to rescue. The Galactic Federation of Light will not implant you with a device that allows you to "hear their voices." They will assist you to open your crown chakra and awaken your Higher Self and increase your ability to access your own God-Self and God consciousness. Confusing the human race about the role of ET's in your development is part of the Family of Dark's agenda.

Vlad knows that humans can't stand confusion and that the

human race seeks pleasure over pain. He believes that if you give humans comfort, easy answers, and help them to avoid pain they will follow you anywhere. Dracula knows that if he can't get you with threats and fear he can always get you with your lower and baser need to please yourself through food, drink, sex and sloth.

VLAD DRACULA: I ONLY CREATED BY MERLIN'S RULES

Merlin is making an argument that the human race is worth saving, and simultaneously he is showing you all what a weak and easily manipulated species you are. If you truly believe in your Darwinian argument which states that the fittest species shall survive, and ultimately rule, then you can't listen to him when he pleads, "Please have mercy on my weak and poorly made species. Please forget all I taught you about adaptability of a species and the natural order of selection, and don't kill off my human race."

You are beginning to see that Merlin is merely making a case for the continuation of a completely inferior species—which by the way makes our roles reversed. See how he likes it. I made such a case to him when he removed the dinosaurs from the Earth. Merlin is fine with karma until he is the beneficiary of it. Now his species is about to be taken off the planet Earth and he is reduced to pleading with me for mercy. You've got to love it! Ironic isn't it?

MERLIN: The human race was not designed as an inferior species, and it is only because of what you did to it that it is "inferior."

VLAD DRACULA: It is only because of what they _allowed_ to have done to them since they are an inferior species you mean. That doesn't prove anything. Their allowance to be dominated and controlled is merely another argument for their inferiority and hence their need to be eradicated by the Creator God—me.

MERLIN: They allowed nothing. Your conquests to destroy and tinker with creation caused their "dumbing down."

VLAD DRACULA: Oh, I see. Now, you are saying that people are not responsible for their own experiences. Which is it, Old Man? Are people Masters or Victims? You love to talk about their mastery—that they are miniature Co-creator Gods themselves—but once again I state the obvious. Merlin doesn't hold to his beliefs when it doesn't suit him. My dinosaurs were victims to his tinkering.

MERLIN: I did not tinker with your dinosaurs; I merely removed them to a more suitable location where they could evolve separately from other species. Besides, the Milky Way was not your Galaxy to play with as you wanted to; you were a student who was invited to create within my domain. You seemed to have forgotten that.

VLAD DRACULA: I only created by your rules, Merlin. I created a superior species and you couldn't handle it. End of story.

MERLIN:
THE ORION WARS CONTINUE

After the invasion of the Andromedan galaxy and the creation of Vlad's senior army officers, he moved outward once again. The Arcturians are extremely isolationist by nature. They do not venture out much. For the most part they take a hands-off approach, even though they have been willing to join the Family of Light and use their massive motherships as ports to rest, repair or refuel, and re-establish vibrational harmony for beings who are in need.

The Arcturians are a peaceful species and they were created by a Creator God to be an experiment in harmonious self-regulation. Unlike the Earth, that was designed to create harmony by the balance of natural order, and outside regulation, the Arcturian star system was designed to achieve natural order by self-regulation. The Earth was designed to achieve balance by different species bringing about the regulation for one another by agreement, harmony and balance—through support such as plants and herbs, water and air—and also by causing death. The Earth was originally designed so that all beings would help one another to live and die thus creating dependence on, and respect for, one another.

In the Arcturus star system the idea was that the species would regulate itself. In other words, decisions about life and death, balance, and natural order would be decided by the individual. An Arcturian decides for themselves, based on what is best for the all, when to reproduce and when to expire. There is no lion chasing down a gazelle; no bacteria eating away a rotting carcass. There is also not nearly as much life on Arcturus as there is on Earth. Earth's plethora of life required quite different means of achieving balance. Arcturians always consider the greater good of all first when making a decision for themselves, and gratefully serve the idea of a community.

News of what Vlad Dracula was doing had reached the Arcturians, and to avoid contamination they decided to ascend to a fifth and sixth dimensional frequency and "close the doors" and quarantine, just as had been done in the angelic realms. Because Vlad Dracula operates only in the lower dimensions, the Arcturians understood that if they raised their vibrational frequency above that of the lower astral (third and fourth dimensions), they would be essentially invisible to Dracula's army.

They felt that the danger of fear being spread to their people was becoming too close at hand, and they made a choice to allow only those who could reach a higher level of consciousness to continue on their planet. They decided that any being who wished to express their individuality, before the good of the people, would be cast out. This was done to keep their planet self-regulating and on an even keel; for they had evolved to the point that they believed the creation of individuated ego was the downfall of any species. The Arcturians looked very similar to one another prior to the quarantine, but after the "doors were closed" appearance self-regulation became extreme, so that there is currently little differentiation between Arcturians on the physical level.

Vlad stepped in just as the beings that were sent away from the Arcturian planet were looking for a new home. They became what you call today, the Grays. The Grays were moved to Zeta Reticuli, and unfortunately, Vlad did not allow them to evolve naturally as would have suited their species the best. Vlad and his officers saw an opportunity to capture and control these beings and use them for their purposes. Any possibility for them to reproduce on their own was taken from them, and they became members of the reptilian army.

Vlad decided that the unemotional aspects of the Andromedans could be paired with the Arcturian belief in serving the greater good so that the Grays could be used as slaves to serve him. Most of them were confused and feeling lost because of the "cast out" scenario, and it was a perfect time for him to recruit and rewire them for his purposes.

This scenario is similar to the fallen angels. Vlad talked to the fallen angels and told them about the evil Merlin who had cast them out of heaven by closing the doors to them. It was easy to recruit them, and there are many fallen angels on the Earth and throughout the universe who want nothing more than to exact their revenge on me and my followers because of what Vlad has told them.

I must interject that the need for quarantine is a desperate measure and undertaken only in extreme circumstances. No one would have been quarantined if Vlad had not started his reign of terror.

VLAD DRACULA: WHY THE QUARANTINE WAS ENACTED

The quarantine was done, by Merlin, to keep the human race from acquiring the knowledge they needed to empower themselves. Most of you have heard that the human race, and the Earth itself, were quarantined to keep your violence away from the rest of the galaxy. Well, if you believe Merlin then you believe that the galaxy had already experienced violence, and so why then quarantine the Earth? Merlin quarantined the Earth to keep you lower "dumbed down" humans from knowing the truth of what happened to you, and to keep you from infecting the rest of his precious galaxy.

I have no problem with you all knowing and understanding that you are an inferior species and completely controlled and owned by both myself and my army. Why would I? I want you to understand how much more powerful my hybrid reptilian and robotic creations are. Again you have been hood-winked by Merlin the (*Ha Ha*) Powerful. Who has the history of quarantining against other beings, me or Merlin?

MERLIN: THE GAME OF LIFE

This dialogue is designed to give all of you who read this the opportunity to experience both sides and to think about good and evil from a different point of view. If each and everything is reflected within each one of you, then only by bringing light to all sides of an issue can you reflect the truth. It has been decided that the human race must begin to enter a phase of mastery that requires them to understand and become responsible for their actions. This is much like a child and a parent relationship, at some point the parent says to the child, "If you hit your friend and grab their toys you will suffer a consequence." At some point the children need to grow up. It is also true that at some point the children have to learn about the outside world.

It is true that you are playing a game; a game of life. Many of you have this information lodged somewhere in your memory banks, and that is why your books and fairy tales repeat these stories over and over again. After all, the mythology that Saint George slays the dragon comes from somewhere. And yet with all these repeated images—the banners of dragons and lions, the stories of vampires and angels—you refuse to believe that they are founded in truth. You believe that *Lord of the Rings* and *Harry Potter* are simply stories that haven't a grain of truth. You believe that Milton's *Paradise Lost* is merely a strange poem. You believe that when the *Book of Revelations* says that Satan is the dragon it is a metaphor. You believe in your world of skyscrapers, tanks, bombs, subways, banks and highways and say that these are real to you, but you fool yourselves that these are the only truth; and this is want Vlad wants. The best way for him to keep the Luciferian deception alive is to make you believe that he is a Disney-like cartoon character, so that anyone who asserts that he is an actual being that has an agenda, will be laughed at and ridiculed.

Do not listen to what he says when he tells you that he wants to be revealed. He only wants you to know what suits him. The Family of Dark will argue that they always state their intentions clearly, but you are too stupid to understand. Vlad tells you that he wants you to know all about him, but he keeps the information coded. The Family of Dark gains power through their secret societies, and they do their business behind dark curtains. They want the shades to stay down and they go to great lengths to keep them drawn. They make sure that the white witches are burned and the truth tellers are killed. How many whistleblowers are killed? Your history is filled with murdered whistleblowers. If they wanted you to know the truth they wouldn't kill those who speak it.

Vlad's army also attacked the Sirius star system. The Sirians, who have the elongated heads, are known as the Annunaki. They also come from Nibiru; a cast-off planet from the Sirian star system. Nibiru was launched out of its orbit by the Draconians during an invasion, and initially used as a docking station by them. Nibiru has changed hands a few times, and has since become an odd mish-mosh of beings, many of whom stay to themselves in isolated colonies on the planet. Nibiru has suffered much.

The Annunaki, contrary to popular belief, are not all bad. The Annunaki are another enslaved, genetically-corrupted species. Not all Annunaki are aligned with the reptilian agenda. They are much like the humans; some work for Dracula and have reptilian allegiances, and have been inbred with the reptilian race, and others work for the Family of Light. There are, however, Annunaki reptilian hybrids.

The Sirians are extremely ancient and wise. They understand the building blocks of life, sacred geometry and how to time travel and alter matter. The Sirians influenced much of life in ancient Egypt. The Sphinx is the blending of man and lion—Osiris—and the representation of these two Christed templates. Osiris ruled as a Lion King in the Sirian system and as a man on Earth. If you understand the Christed template of Aslan as the Christed Lion, and Osiris as the Christed human, you see that the Sphinx is a blend of these two templates.

The template of the cat is an ancient one and is found in many places. Although it arose out of the multiple star system of Lyra it is seeded throughout many galaxies. Cat people populate the Regulus star system as well, and they also suffered greatly when they were attacked by the reptilian army. The Cat people, on the multiple star system of Regulus, are half human/half cat. The Regulans were also attacked and suffered in the Orion Wars.

The historical Jesus was a Starseed. He was (among other things) a Pleiadian being who had experienced incarnations throughout time and space. His Pleiadian insights and understandings were only some of the ones he brought to Earth. He brought knowledge, "miraculous" gifts, and a deep compassion for the enslavement that humans endure. Jesus attacked the moneylenders, because he knew, like today, that it is often the greedy moneylenders who hoard the wealth like dragons. This is why he said that it is easier for a camel to get through the eye of a needle than a rich man to get into heaven. He knew the wealthy bankers were working to get rich on the backs of the honest man. Jesus was an activist. Jesus was not only a man of words but a man of action. He boldly lived his truth, even to his death.

Jesus knew the secrets of the advanced civilizations, and he knew how to turn water into wine. Jesus was a wizard like Merlin and Harry Potter. Like many of you have been in different incarnations. Why then have you lost your abilities? First because they were taken from you by the reptilian overlords; and then because your vibrations became so dense that you couldn't sustain the gifts nor even be trusted to hold them.

During the time of Atlantis many wizards, who remembered having the gifts to create miracles like Jesus or Moses did, began to reclaim their power; and then they became power mad. Wizard wars occur when Starseeds utilize their gifts to destroy or overpower an enemy wizard. The solar system shows evidence of these wars. Mars was destroyed by wizards fighting one another in the Orion wars. Mars was (among other things) an Annunaki outpost—Niburians used Mars as a stationary home and place of operations. It originally was more than the barren rock you see today. It held life. When the Annunaki decided to come to the Earth and colonize it for themselves they used Mars to launch from. The heads on Easter Island were designed to gaze upon and honor those who lived on Mars. As human beings wake up to their true history they will begin to understand that the planets in their solar system have long and complex histories as well.

VLAD DRACULA: MERLIN AS THE EVIL GOD

Okay, wait a minute here. There have got to be rules to this discussion and one of the rules has to be to let me speak in my defense. There have been thousands of years of damaging material designed to destroy and slight me; at least give me time for my defense.

You have been propagandized by Merlin's army. Read the Bible and put Merlin's name in place of the word God. How many times does it tell you to fear an angry and vengeful God? Most certainly the God of your Bible does not love you unconditionally. The God of your Bible loves you if you behave the way he wants you to behave. Or should I say, the angry and vengeful Merlin loves you only when you behave according to his rules? Merlin himself has admitted that he created the Earth. Merlin himself has told you he is a Creator *God*. So, when the Bible goes on and on about how God punished Job or God destroyed this town or those people, it is speaking about Merlin, not me.

God made Adam and Eve. Merlin told you *he* made Adam and Eve; so he is God. That should shake you to the core and make you not trust him. The Bible was written by a bunch of confused men who didn't have a clue what the hell was happening to them. They lived in fear of punishment from a wicked and vengeful God (Merlin), and in their confusion and need to explain the events of their lives; they wrote the stories as well as they could. But one fact truly stands out, and that is that mankind was punished and fearful of what God would do to them.

Mankind looked to the heavens to see if God was about to punish them. Mankind made human sacrifices to appease the wicked and evil God that they feared. Is that Merlin or me? Ask yourself that. Who has done the most damage and instilled the most fear in mankind. Read the Bible and the answer becomes clear: Merlin/God.

"Behold, I will command," says the Lord, "and will bring them back to this city; and they will fight against it and take it and burn it with fire. I will make the cities of Judah a desolation without inhabitant."

Or

Just read the Book of Job.

MERLIN: FALLEN ANGEL GODS

People who lived in fear of the "gods" lived in fear of Vlad's reptilian invaders who had returned to the Earth to recapture it. This is why the theme of reptilian "gods" and overlords is repeated throughout the world. Many ancient civilizations worshipped dragons, snakes or lizard-like creatures—those were the controllers that had to be appeased. It was not me that the people feared and revered. It was these beings. Even today Asian cultures revere the dragons. As for the Bible, I will say read the Bible and interpret it as you will. That is an argument no one ever wins. The lesson of Job was originally designed to talk to you about reincarnation and karma, but after the concept of reincarnation was stricken from the Bible, it became a fable about how unfair life was; and how unforgiving God was.

The fallen angels have fascinated mankind for eons, and stories of them are woven into the traditions of every culture. It is important, as you consider these beings, that you remember your brain is already wired and imprinted with opinions and beliefs from previous lives and childhood. When someone tries to put a different spin on a piece of information you automatically resist it, because it makes you uncomfortable. You resist it and come up with a myriad of reasons why that person is not only wrong; but even at times evil or has devious intentions. That makes you comfortable again.

Everyone on the Earth struggles to be safe. Survival and comfort are supreme motivators. Some believe peace will make them safe, and others believe war is the route to safety. The motivation is the same and merely the path changes. You sense intuitively that your feet are already on tenuous ground and any bit of solid information, especially if it supports what your parents, teachers, politicians and priests have told you, whether it is true or not, comes as a comfort. Those who preach to the masses, lie and manipulate, know this and use it to their advantage. For example, how many preachers or politicians have told you to pray to Jesus for salvation and monetary assistance while they took great quantities of money out of your pockets? "Give me your money—I know you are hurting financially—pray to Jesus to get more money."

This confusion, created by those who work for Vlad and his army, has left you powerless and unable to discern any bit of truth for yourselves. As was stated at the opening, this information is not given to you to tell you what your truth should be, but to stimulate the truth that resides within you. As Masters and Co-Creator gods you are responsible for your own truth.

The fallen angels became trapped at the time of the quarantine of the third and fourth dimensions from the higher dimensions, and there are a number of reasons they became trapped. Some of them became trapped because they had been trying to reach down and assist beings who were becoming overwhelmed with fear. The dense vibrations became too much and they were overcome. Some became trapped because they aligned with Vlad Dracula and believed his story that he was the true and rightful heir to this kingdom. Still others allowed curiosity to draw them near.

As you have been told, fallen angels created the first dragon races. Their bodies solidified into dragons and these are the Ancient Ones. The tendency is to lump everyone and everything into categories. This makes it easier for the human mind to digest this information, but it is far from accurate.

The Earth's history is varied, and no one story covers all the truth. When beings from the multiple star systems of the Pleiades arrived on Earth they lived in the fairy realms—their bodies were not as dense as the Earth humans. The Earth became a melting pot for many beings throughout the galaxy; some searching for another home, an escape from the Orion wars and others looking for another planet to control and dominate. The Pleiadians, who managed to escape the reptilian siege of their planet, were homeless; many came to the Earth.

Although they had human template bodies, Pleiadians were much less dense than you know humans to be today. In the Pleiades, they were part angel and part human, and they were created as an experiment to see if angels and humans could co-exist; as a result they lived in the fifth, sixth and even seventh dimensions. They sang, danced, played and were joyful beings of light whose bodies were designed to mirror the perfected human template. They developed the arts and they enjoyed the gifts of moving freely through space—what you think of as teleportation. Because there was no fear, there was no danger of misuse of their gifts, and for a long time the Pleiadians had the "best of both worlds." Pleiadians enjoyed the creational abilities of the Co-Creator gods. Many Starseeds have Pleiadian memories. Many long to go home to the Pleiades and regain the life of joy they once had.

What is most interesting about the Pleiadians is that their society—which was quite different from the Arcturians—mostly closely resembled a hive of bees. There were Queen Bees whose job it was to hold the vibrational frequency of the planet at a high enough level that the angelic existence could be maintained by the hive. So, instead of each individual Pleiadian being responsible for their own vibrational frequency, they had Queen Bees to do it for them. And, just like in a hive of bees, the Queen was tended to by servants who made sure that the Queen did not have to trouble herself with daily tasks. This type of existence was re-created by the ancient temple priestesses who were kept in isolation and catered to in order that they would stay pure and be able to connect directly to the gods and bring wisdom to the masses.

The Pleiades was one of the last star systems to fall to the Draconian siege. Because the Pleiadians were living primarily on the higher dimensions they were immune to the ravages taking place on the third and fourth. It wasn't until word of what was happening to the angelic realms, and the other star systems, reached their ears that they began to have a consciousness that lowered their vibrational state. It started slowly, and hell didn't enter heaven all at once on the Pleiades, but once they had heard of the Orion Wars the collective vibration began to lower. Fear lowers the vibration of any being, and even the smallest touch of fear reaching one of the Queen Bees was enough to spread it to the hive in small increments.

It wasn't until the Pleiades lowered its vibration enough, and a fourth dimensional signal was sent out, that it could be picked up by the Draconians. The Draconian siege of the Pleiades was swift and merciless. They came onto the planet in ships and they took these innocents by complete surprise. Many of the Pleiadians were unable to process what was happening to them because they had known only love, joy and peace. When they were overpowered by these fierce reptilian beings they didn't even know how to feel as fear was a foreign emotion to them. The crash was swift and sudden.

The Queen Bees were considered to be quite the prize to the conquering army. These individuals were the first to be captured and enslaved, but they were not killed. It was clear to the Andromedan scientists that they were to be studied and integrated into the "fold." Vlad Dracula had given very specific instructions to his officers: Those beings not useful to the reptilian hunt for DNA perfection were to be destroyed immediately, and those who were useful were to be captured and harvested. If you recall, the Andromedan scientists were fascinated with perfected systems, and these Queen Bees represented the perfected Pleiadian vision.

You could say that the Queen Bee model was the downfall of the Pleiadian people. Because they hadn't learned to hold their frequency high as individuals, and were reliant upon someone outside of themselves to keep their frequencies lifted, they were lost once they lost the Queen. As a result, once the Queens fell, all the others fell immediately.

The Andromedan reptilian officers saw quite quickly that these beings were able to do with their bodies what the Andromedans had only been able to accomplish through their machines. Even though the reptilians had become quite advanced through the co-opting of the Andromedan DNA, and learning how to create advanced devices and means of travel, it was astonishing to them to see a civilization where certain individuals could maintain such a high frequency that they could control the rest of the civilization.

They saw the possibilities inherent in this type of frequency control, and the Queen Bees were the top prize. The first thing they did was to attempt a mating with these beings. It was believed that if the Draconian reptilian DNA was merged with the Pleiadian DNA it would produce beings that could hold and control frequencies with their bodies and create a kind of natural mind control. They also believed that it would increase the ability of the Draconians to travel in the astral plane (without ships) and give them the ability to do many "tricks" that had eluded them. Vibrational states were artificially introduced into the Queen's body through the use of machines, and changes were observed. Obviously, the Eden-like existence was destroyed, but scientists found a way to alter a body's vibrational state, not by making you feel good inside (as is reproduced on the Earth in meditation) but by artificial means.

It is because of the Pleiadian DNA snatching that the reptilians began to understand the notion of shapeshifting. They later used it with the Antarean star system DNA to allow them to move between the human form and the reptilian form. The reptilians are masters of shapeshifting, in part, because they studied the Pleiadian methods of using the mind to alter matter at will. The ability they have to move from third to fourth dimension began with the understandings they gained from the Pleiadians. It also contributed to their ability to torture their captives by inserting frequencies into the mind. One of the favorite ways to kill an enemy is to send vibrations into the mind that drive the person crazy; and then put the weapon into their hand that they will use to commit suicide.

VLAD DRACULA: MY CASE AGAINST THE PLEIADIANS

The Pleiadians were living in La-La land and they still do. It is because of the Pleiadians that you have many of the lies swirling around you today on the Earth. The Pleiadians have their heads in the sand, and they always have. Besides they are supremely selfish. It's true that I co-opted the only useful gifts the Pleiadians had, but as a species overall they are useless and will bring about the downfall of any civilization they put their hands upon. They are notorious for their shapeshifting ways; they appear good but will change to evil at the blink of an eye.

They have huge egos. They need to be the top of the heap. Ask yourselves why all the artists you know have huge egos? It is because of their Pleiadian roots. They believe that everyone should be worshipping and adoring them. They are intolerant and short-tempered. Be honest, you know it's true.

They think they are better than everyone else—their love of beauty is to blame for all the botox in the world. They can't stand things to be ugly. They care more about trees and flowers, elves and fairies than they do people. They hate the human race and consider them inferior, and yes they always want to go home to their beloved planet and get the hell off this inferior one. Being a member of the Earth human race is a shadow of themselves they can barely tolerate.

They are masters at denial. They will pretend anything to feel better, and curse anyone who won't play their game of "let's pretend."

They hate growing old. They hate being trapped in the inferior human body. They hate reptilians with a passion because they are ugly (in their minds). The only Pleiadians that have any respect for the reptilians are those who have made peace with the DNA splicing that was done on them. And how many of those do you know? And, yes, I did DNA splice them and harvest them, but I made a very inferior species much, much better. The more reptilian DNA a Pleiadian has the better they are; tougher and smarter.

Isn't that the natural order of things, Merlin?

MERLIN: WHAT HE DIDN'T STEAL HE DESTROYED

Human Pleiadians struggle to hold their frequency high on the Earth, because they are learning to do for themselves what previously had been done by Queen Bees. The Earth is a good training ground for the Pleiadian soul, because it teaches them self-reliance when it comes to being responsible for keeping their own energy lifted.

ALPHA CENTAURI

The centaurs come from Alpha Centauri. These are the horse-people. The back half is the horse and the front half is human. They have arms and are quite intelligent, but they also have the swiftness of a horse. These Alpha Centaurians are a fierce, proud and independent breed. Although quite kind by nature they are also very strong-willed. They are warriors who will go down fighting to remain sovereign.

When the reptilian armies attacked Alpha Centauri they found these beings ready to do battle. The centaurs had been warned by the Galactic Federation that the Draconians were advancing upon them, but they were a proud bunch who wanted to fight the reptilians on their own. The Council of War pleaded with them to take aid, but the most they could convince the centaurs to do was to signal for help if they appeared to be losing the battle. Against the advice of counsel—including my own—the centaurs prepared to do battle alone.

Although fierce and cunning, the centaurs were quickly overwhelmed. The Andromedan-reptilian officer in charge informed Vlad that these beings appeared to be quite headstrong and it would present a problem to tame them. Vlad ordered them divided in half—the human from the horse—to weaken them and create suffering. Unlike other species, he deconstructed the centaurs and cast them out to suffer. He did not pilfer their DNA as he felt it was no use to him, but he wanted to make sure they would never fight against him again. A few of the centaurs escaped to the Earth, and reports of their existence abound in ancient texts, but these were all male, and once the third dimensional template for their species had been destroyed they could not reproduce.

They are extinct and their template remains now on the fourth and fifth dimension only, having been eradicated from the third. Human-centaurs from Alpha Centauri have certain commonalities just as other Starseeds do. Although not as well known on the Earth as some of the others, such as Pleiadian, Arcturian or Sirian, the centaurs do exist on the Earth, but now they are chopped in half and disempowered.

Horses on the Earth are all that is left of the back end of the half horse/half man. They have been used, and often times abused by humans, most of who do not understand or appreciate the deep sorrow, wisdom and longing that exists within them. Many humans who have unconscious memories of their life upon Alpha Centauri serve as horse whisperers and long to give their "other half" the respect and love they deserve. Many horse lovers will tell you that they feel most complete when they are riding or just being with their horse. Animals reincarnate as humans do, and often a horse and a rider will re-find themselves as they seek out their other half.

Most human ex-centaurs have deep sorrow and rage within them, and they are angry at the system that enslaves them. Although they feel incomplete, searching for something they long forgot they were, they often retain the emotional qualities of their centaurian heart. It can be very difficult for a centaurian-human to trust. They tend to have wary personalities and like to be alone, for it is alone that they truly feel safe.

Vlad has destroyed many species, but the half horse/half human is greatly missed. The Creator Gods look forward to the time when centaurs will agree to re-establish their template upon the Earth and throughout the galaxy, for then we know that peace has returned.

VLAD DRACULA: THE CENTAURS

There is barely a shred of truth to that bit of war history. We gave the centaurs the opportunity to surrender. We offered peace in exchange for surrender. We often offer the option of surrender to a species willing to acknowledge our right to control them. It is not our pleasure to destroy a species, but any species that is so stubborn that they will not agree to live with us is obviously looking for a fight. That was the centaurs. They made it very clear that their objective was to kill as many of us as possible. They made it very clear that surrender was not an option for them. I warned them what was in store for them. I told them that if they would surrender we would not kill them, and that we merely needed to use their planet as a base of operation. We weren't even interested in them as a species per se. We wanted the land to work from. We needed bases in that sector of the universe. We were going to herd the centaurs into an area agreed upon by both parties, and we would take the rest of the land.

I was even willing to let them be. I said, "We offer you the opportunity to survive in exchange of use of your lands. We don't care about you, and we know how independent you are, and that you do not want to join any team in this war. We know you will not join with Merlin's army and fight against us if we leave you alone." But, they refused to listen. They were unwilling to give, and so I destroyed them as any general is forced to do. I knew if I left them to their devices they would continually wage war against my bases.

My "deconstructing them" was merely a defense to disempower

them. It was Merlin who tried to save them by offering them a home on the Earth. He is the one who took the horses to the Earth and manifested them there. He is the one who offered the centaurian men and women a home. I had no need of them once I knew they had been disenfranchised and disempowered.

If you are a centaur who is unhappy with being on the Earth blame Merlin, he brought you there.

MERLIN: THE FALLEN ANGELS AND BETELGEUSE

The Betelgeuse star system serves as a portal for the fallen angel demonic beings. The fallen angels who aligned with Vlad, and agreed to work in the fourth dimension, needed a way to move inter-dimensionally throughout the universe. Betelgeuse is their home, and their portal to other worlds. Betelgeuse houses the most depraved fourth dimensional demons you can imagine. The Vampire Fallens make their home there, for example. So do many other demonic beings including: The Grey Mists that Suck Souls, the Organ Harvesting Demonics, the Carrion Demonics, the Black Siege Demonics who create plagues, and the demonic leadership that rules all of the above known as the Dark Triad. They constantly battle amongst themselves, especially if they have their eye on someone or something and another demon challenges their territory.

Because none of these demons know how to receive nourishment from Light they all must feed off of other living things, and are parasitic by nature. They are all good friends to Vlad Dracula. Many contracts have been made between these groups—some broken—and punishment has been swift. Power struggles erupt occasionally. Early on the Dark Triad challenged Dracula's hold over the third and fourth dimensions, but Dracula's reputation for repudiation caused them to back down and join forces, and so far they have not co-opted his position as Supreme Leader. Vlad Dracula is the only one who has managed to enlist both the third and the fourth dimensional armies, and use both to his advantage. None of the other Family of Dark members has an army that can move into both the third and fourth dimension. Vlad's reptilians, and his extended demonic family, keep him supreme. The Dark Triad has no power over the reptilians, and Vlad Dracula insists that they keep the Betelgeuse demonic energies out of his way unless he calls them into service.

When Vlad needs to psychically attack someone, in order to weaken them, he will enlist the services of these demonic beings that will use the Betelgeuse portal to visit the one they are assigned to attack. Grey Mists are used to bring individuals to despair, often urging them to commit suicide. The Organ Harvesters are used to gather useful DNA and body parts after the demise of an individual; if the person is a prime candidate for harvesting they will often find a means to kill them first by joining forces with the Grey Mists.

The Black Siege Demonics are responsible for the parasitic illnesses that kill off many people—the Black Plague being the most famous but by no means the only. The Carrions are there to take away the souls that have sold themselves to Vlad Dracula. They always bring them directly back to Vlad. He rewards the Carrions with food, but they are not allowed to harm the individual they are retrieving. "Bring them back whole," is what Vlad tells them.

That's enough for now. You get the picture.

The major portal entry and exit is located directly below the Vatican. It has branches that extend all over the world, but the main Betelgeuse portal lies there. The Vatican was built on this site because it was believed that by harnessing the Betelgeuse portal the Vatican authorities could direct these demonic beings toward their enemies. The Roman Catholic Church believed that the Demonics would be at their beck and call and would do their bidding. They knew they were harnessing a powerful energy that could assist them in destroying those who opposed them.

What can be done to defend oneself from these beings? Their biggest weakness is that they can't see anything above the fourth dimension, so if you are able to sustain a fifth dimensional (or higher) vibration you are invisible to them. It is for this reason they can be very good teachers because they push you to raise your vibrational frequency higher in your attempt to escape them.

The Demonics are very angry and frustrated by the fact that they can be eluded by this vibrational lift and it is for this reason that Vlad and company have designed many devices to keep your frequencies low so that they can find you. Most of your modern "conveniences" are enslavement devices that lower your vibrational frequency and keep you on the radar. Cell towers, television, movies, videos and other types of equipment are all being utilized to keep your vibration low enough that you can't escape the grasp of these beings. Hunger, physical pain and disease are also means they have developed to keep you at their mercy.

Most humans are innocent and have no knowledge or understanding of the complexity of this war. They are easily preyed upon by the Demonic Fallen Angels, all of whom are vampires in some manner or another. Humans provide an easy and tasty treat for these beings, and they need the human race to supply them with energetic food.

Addiction is one of the most effective ways to keep a human being around as a food source. Addicts are always attached onto by a Betelgeuse demonic entity in the fourth dimension, and the addiction is so hard to break because the human must not only break themselves off the addiction, but the demonic attachment as well. It is for this reason that the addict becomes drained of life and often returns to the addictive behavior.

When an individual agrees to give their soul to Vlad in exchange for power, fame, or money (or all three) one or more of these Betelgeuse Demonics is assigned to them. The demonic reports back to the Dark Triad on the behavior of the human; Vlad is not bothered with each and every action of each possessed human unless they start to cause him trouble. The only humans that Vlad Dracula takes a special and personal interest in are those on either team—Family of Light or Family of Dark—who are having a large impact on the human race.

In order to be truly effective as a Family of Light member it will be essential that you meet Vlad Dracula "face-to-face" and overcome your fear of him. This is what Jesus was doing in the desert when he met with the Devil. Jesus said to Vlad, "Give me everything you've got, Devil. Throw it all at me and lift me to my Christed Self. For only when I can overcome my fear of you, and free myself of your temptations, will I be truly free to do my work as my Christed Self."

Most people want to breeze past this part of Jesus' life and training because it frightens them; but it is very important information. Jesus was teaching you that you will never be free unless you overcome all fear, and that includes fear of the darkest of the dark—the Devil himself. Most humans want to run from this, thinking they can free themselves by only looking at the light side of humanity. But, Jesus lived as he did to show human beings each and every step they needed to take to be free from fear and become Christed. Those who say they are not afraid of the Devil, but haven't done the work to become free of that energy, are merely naïve. Jesus knew enough to be afraid, but he knew that he had to overcome that level of fear and darkness to find the highest Light.

One of the biggest mistakes the Family of Dark made was not hiding the story of Jesus wrestling with the Devil. It is one of their deepest regrets. If they had told you that all you need to do is look toward the Light to free yourself, you would still feel chained by fear and temptation at every moment, and you would blame yourself for feeling bad.

Throughout the Bible the instances where Jesus acts from his human self are designed to give you hope. They allow you to know that nobody is perfect and even Jesus had to wrestle with the Devil. Jesus showed you to confront the Devil to free yourself from his grasp. There are many teachers alive today who want you to run as fast as you can from the dark, but these teachers want you to live in fear of the dark. The true teacher will tell you to turn and face your fear, for only then will you be free.

The darkness is counting on you not looking in its direction, and that is the way it will keep a hold of you. If you don't know how the Family of Dark operates, and you don't understand the nature of demonic energies that attach to you parasitically, then you can't release yourself from them. Raise your frequency with your release from fear. Then you will realize how little power they truly have—they need *you* to survive and if you don't let them, they will die. How powerful is that?

VLAD DRACULA: THE DEMONICS

The Demonics love their work, by the way. The Demonics are happy. How many humans are happy?

The Demonics enjoy their life; they enjoy the manner in which they feed and they enjoy serving both me and the Dark Triad. Everything is their Source of Nourishment. Where is this God that Merlin speaks of that supplies food and nourishment to Jesus and the rest of you deluded humans? Where is your God? Look around you at your world. It is a world of parasites.

If it is as above so below, perhaps your God is a parasitic God feeding off of you. Did you ever consider that?

MERLIN: VLAD DRACULA AND THE NAZI AGENDA

Here you all are in the 21st century and you are trying to understand how this history—millions of years old now—affects you.

Since the beginning, the only reason anyone aligns with Vlad is because they believe that is where the true power lies. They believe that he is holding truth and power. Those who have been victimized by others make good recruits as well. People who feel helpless and hopeless will often want to join the Family of Dark because it makes them feel empowered. Who do you think spread the rumor that you could be "kicked out of heaven?" You guessed it, Vlad. Why? To get people on his team. The thinking goes, 'You're lost anyway, so why not join the team with the power? The team that won't abandon you…'

It appears then that people choose sides hoping to get some power behind them, and they believe that they will be safe with the side they have chosen. Remember, people are motivated by safety. If they choose voodoo and black magic, it is to be safe; if they choose God and Light it is because they believe it will keep them safe. And don't think that Vlad doesn't know how to use that to motivate someone to join his team. Learning how to feel safe through light and unconditional love can appear to be a long and arduous process, as many spiritual masters have clearly demonstrated. The thought that one can do some incantations and voodoo and be safe is just too tempting. Many people succumb to that. Of course, as I mentioned, they also succumb to base desires that are driven by ego.

You are beginning to understand that there is a connection between the fallen angels and the ET's. You are also beginning to understand that the fallen angels are the ETs. They are the dragons, the reptilians, the Pleiadians, and since all beings in some sense "fell into density," everyone you know is, by definition, a fallen angel.

First and foremost it is important to understand that much of what was written in the Bible, especially in the Book of Enoch, about the Nephilim being the children of the fallen angels, and their mating with humans, is in fact written about what you would think of as ETs. By the time that Enoch wrote his work, the fallen angels had long become the dragons, and Vlad was already on his way to re-taking the Earth. So, in actuality, the fallen angels mating with the humans are actually more what you would all call extra-terrestrial mating. The "Fallens" as they are called in the Bible took third dimensional shape in many forms, but could not mate with humans until they had become encased in compatible bodies. Enoch is referring to the DNA experimentation and hybridization that was done to create a "super race." If the idea of "super race" is reminding you of the Nazi agenda you are exactly right—the Nazi agenda is indeed the same exact agenda that has been plaguing the many worlds since Vlad decided to dominate and control the universe. Nazis are members of Vlad's army.

All the mating and DNA corruption is being driven by Vlad Dracula's desire to produce his super reptilian-based race. The objective was to work with Hitler and his generals to create a super race that he could control and manage. WWII taught Vlad that fighting this war on the Earth above ground and openly was a big mistake. Hitler's plan was defeated because Vlad's arrogance brought the reptilian Nazi army to the surface. After WWII the Nazis (with the help of many governments around the world) moved underground. Most of you are aware of Operation Paperclip, the name of the operation to recruit Nazi scientists and bring them to America, as it is now "declassified" information. They have been working in underground laboratories ever since. The agenda remains the same: create a super race and get rid of the undesirable humans. So, you are beginning to see that Vlad has expanded beyond his original ideas millions of years ago to have a race of super reptilians. He has now decided that he must make superior all the races he chooses to keep intact and then own and control them, and that includes the human race.

The human race has been problematic for Vlad. I created humans with a soul template that was not easily reproduced, and it is one of the reasons that being human is considered to be a treasured experience. It has built within it the opportunity for tremendous amounts of self-actualization, self-determination, and self-expression. The soul Matrix is so complex that it cannot be easily reproduced. As a result it has had to be snatched by Vlad and his helpers. They are attempting to insert these snatched souls into robotic/human clones, and then they hope to reproduce these souls in laboratories. You shouldn't doubt it; your scientists working in the light of day have perfected cloning. By eventually reproducing human souls Vlad and his army hope to own and control the human template.

During the 70's and 80's the human Family of Dark, led by neo-Nazi scientists, began their serious work to create a robotic/human race of beings that would be ensouled. Their goal is to integrate them into the human family, and yet find a way to retain control over them. Serious studies were done, and much abduction of innocent humans took place. Mind control experimentation during those decades was at its height, and some of the abductees literally had their souls snatched from their bodies to be utilized to study, and hopefully transplant into robots.

It was first necessary to shut the human organism down to near death levels. Many of you have heard that the soul can be weighed, and that at death the human body loses 21 grams of weight as the soul exits. This led scientists to believe that the soul was an actual thing that could be captured; but first the human had to be killed or brought close to death. A near-death experience was induced. When the soul exited the body, registered by both the weight and also various sensitive electromagnetic instruments, they discovered the method to literally magnetize it and hold it in suspended animation. If you saw one of the rooms where these were held it would radiate intense light and could be seen floating above a pedestal. The soul would appear as dots of light, and each one is as individual as a fingerprint. The soul would remain there until ready for insertion into a robotic creation. Unfortunately for these creations, and the Family of Dark, many of these robotic humans are rejecting the soul implants, and what look like strokes or confusion in an individual, are often the breaking down of these creations.

Those who had their soul snatched either died; or in rare cases remained alive but empty for many years. The reason the scientists wanted the unensouled humans to remain alive was so they could study them and find out how they fared.

THE MATRIX

The human mind is fed by a system known as the Matrix. Each Creator God is responsible for the system that runs their species. The question is not whether you will be hooked into a Matrix, but which Matrix you are going to hook into. Vlad Dracula and his army long ago hacked into my Earth Matrix by laying down another program—or Lower Matrix—to hook you into fear. In order for the Lower Matrix program to be received successfully, Vlad needed to separate the lobes of the brain into two halves, and unplug your DNA from twelve strands to two. He then re-inserted the two-stranded human DNA into this hacked Lower Matrix computer program.

When you are plugged into the Lower Matrix your mind interprets the codes accordingly. In other words you may receive the 333 signals or frequencies, but you won't interpret them the same. Whereas your higher consciousness would interpret 333 as a Pleiadian or Divine Trinity frequency, your lower consciousness will interpret it as a control signal. This is true with every download. The Nazis understood this perfectly. The Swastika was originally a Tibetan Buddhist symbol for goodness and friendship; they turned it around and imprinted it with hatred. Instead of supporting unity and harmony, the symbol supported destruction and fear. Then they hung it everywhere and each time you looked at it now you saw fear and hatred. They essentially re-programmed the Matrix of the Swastika.

It is like a software program. If you are running a Windows software program you will never be able to read MAC. No matter how hard you try to read MAC you can't, it's incompatible, and you don't have the right software. This is what Vlad and his army did to you; they rewrote the program and hooked you into it. Your brain has been unable to receive signals from the original Creator Gods mainframe ever since.

In the 1980s new codes were imprinted and slipped into Vlad's old program to begin to awaken those individuals who were advanced enough to interpret the codes from a higher consciousness perspective. These codes were numerical signals designed to awaken enough people from the dream of the Lower Matrix. 11:11, 333, 444, 1234, 12:12 are just a few of the major codes that stimulated some of the more advanced Starseeds and began to alter their ability to receive information. Enough of the enlightened mind existed in these Starseeds that they could receive the information; they might not have known what it meant, but they knew it was important. It stimulated their consciousness. Over time their memory began to awaken and they were able to interpret the signals. With the entry of these codes into the old Matrix, new information could be received and the individual could begin to "re-member" themselves. Past life information began to re-emerge, metaphysical understanding began to awaken, and the human wake-up call was sounded.

Now those who wanted to preserve the Lower Matrix became afraid of this awakening and began a very vast campaign of disinformation. Most New Agers have been taken in by these campaigns and many lost their way. Vlad Dracula and the Family of Dark have been controlling the computer codes for a long, long time. Because they have been in control, many of them have been awake and knowledgeable about what has been going on.

When they entered the Earth (whether born into the body or, in rare cases, as walk-ins) many of the Starseeds were inserted into the old Matrix. What may be difficult for many of you to understand is that these Starseeds are from the future. They have "come back" in time to alter the future; a future in which humanity, enslaved by Vlad's army, becomes more robot than human. The Starseeds are here to preserve the template of the human soul.

These Family of Light members thought they could sneak in the door by being born to human parents, but then begin to impact the old Matrix from within, and hopefully bust it wide open. The risk was that they would fall too deeply asleep and unfortunately, many of them forgot who they were and they thought they had come to the Earth to live normal lives. They thought that their purpose was the same as the average human; to procreate and make a living doing something they don't really like to do, and try to make it to the finish line called death with a minimal of suffering. Life over and done. *Phew!* That is how powerful the Lower Matrix is. These individuals became so lost in the dream of the Lower Matrix they couldn't wake up. They may feel deep dissatisfaction, but they don't really understand it. Many feel that something big is on the horizon, and they are here to prevent it; but they don't know what to do.

In extreme cases, to avoid the slumber of live human birth a number of "walk-ins" were sent to Earth. These people did not experience human birth, but came in later to assure that they would have a greater chance of staying awake. To walk-in means that a soul exchange has taken place (by agreement) later in life. A human who is about to die will agree to a soul exchange; essentially they go to heaven and a higher vibrational being takes over the body. It allows higher vibrational beings such as angels to enter the Earth and work without having to experience the birth process.

The Family of Dark was very aware of the challenges facing the awakening Starseeds and designed a plan to capture and confuse them, and hopefully either send them scurrying back onto the Lower Matrix, or to make them lose faith in themselves and/or God. The Family of Dark knows that the Family of Light has a natural aversion to darkness and will do whatever they can to avoid it; which suits the Family of Dark just fine. It allows them to work undetected. They knew that most Family of Light members would want to pretend that there are no evil or bad things, and they knew that people who preach these 'don't look at darkness' ideas would attract the Family of Light, and could be used to steer them away from remembering who they were and why they had come to the Earth. They developed the religion called the New Age movement to do just that.

They taught it was more spiritual to forget who you were and you should only be in the "Now. " Certainly there are important metaphysical concepts to be learned by understanding that all moments exist in the Now. This also does not mean that you should fret about the past or the future. Certainly fretting about what has been, or what is to be, will not provide peace. But, unfortunately many of you misinterpreted the concept of living in the Now to mean that you should forget the past. If this is so then "those who forget history are destined to repeat it." It also means you will dishonor your vision of the future; the future you are here to impact.

Remembering fully who it is you are throughout time and space is your right and privilege as Co-Creator gods. In tribal communities knowledge of who you were was passed down through the oral traditions of the shamans. It was the job of the shaman to be the storyteller and keeper of ancient wisdom for the tribe. Who keeps this wisdom for all of you now? Your television programs and your movies have become your shamans. But, you have no context within which to place the images and stories that come to you, and most of you relegate them to fiction, and neatly push them under the rug, still wondering who it is you are. It is because of this destruction of your collective memory that certain religious leaders have been able to reduce human history down to merely a few thousand years; the better to keep you asleep and unaware of your mystical and spiritual roots.

Vlad Dracula and his team convinced many of you that anyone who had metaphysical insights had to be a member of the Family of Light. They told you that if someone put out a shingle with the words, Sacred, Light, Nurture, or Spirit that you could trust them to steer you to the "right place." That the Galactic Federation would rescue you and that you didn't have to do anything. All you have to do is just wait for them to come and get you. They taught you that you shouldn't look at what was happening around you and ignore anything that makes you uncomfortable. Only look at the good and push away anything that doesn't make you feel good at every moment.

Oh yes, they also taught that only special people can access God or angels—and you are probably not one of them. They told you that if someone tells you that a book comes from Jesus or Buddha then it's good and you should revere them and give them your power. In other words it became another religion to disempower the masses, make them doubt their ability to find Truth within themselves, and forget that they have direct access to God and their Higher Matrix. They wanted you to forget that you can plug-in directly and don't need anyone else to do it for you. They feared you remembering that you can plug yourself into the Higher Matrix so much that they created guru after guru to make sure you search everywhere outside of yourself for empowerment. And all the time the answer was within you.

The New Age Movement became big business. Billions of dollars were made by false prophets. This does not mean that there are not well-intentioned and gifted spiritual leaders among you. But, how can you tell the difference when you are lost and confused and cut off from your own truth? Preachers are everywhere, but how many of them tell you that you don't really need them to find God or truth? Very few want to help you to walk on your own. "This too and more shall ye do," a true teacher will say. A true leader wants you to walk on water all by yourself. When you are awake to your history you will no longer need anyone else to tell you who it is you are. You will awaken to the truth of your own soul's path. "Re-member" means just that; putting back together the pieces of yourself.

VLAD DRACULA: MEMBERS OF THE FAMILY OF LIGHT ARE WHINING BABIES

My biggest problem with the Family of Light is that they are all whiners and complainers and the only reason they are so unhappy is that they are losing the Big Game. And yes, it is a game. There is no doubt about that fact. We are on an enormous chessboard and we are playing the game of "Life." I have you all in checkmate; it's the eleventh hour and you are all quite upset that you are about to lose everything.

Yes, I was clever. Yes, I deceived you and took advantage of your innocence and naïveté. I will full well admit that. But, it's because I'm smarter than you are, and I'm smarter than Merlin. I'm smarter than all the other Creator Gods. They are losing, they are pissed, and they want you all to side with them against me.

You all agreed to play this Big Game. You all agreed to fall from grace; take on third dimensional bodies and enter the fray. You knew the rules. You knew that it was going to get tough; but you did it anyway. And why? You agreed to play because this game of duality is fascinating. The game of dark and light has become an addiction.

You are all gamblers in the Game of Life, and you all think that next time it's going to be you who will win. "The Family of Light will be victorious!" you holler. If that isn't dualistic thinking with a winner and loser, I don't know what is. You think you are so much better than I am, but are you really? So far you've been losing a lot and you are pissed, and you want me to back off and even the score board. So, let me say that from my perspective you are a bunch of poor sports. At this point I am like the House in Las Vegas, but you keep on throwing me your chips.

Now, let's simplify this to words you can all understand. You love the computer hackers that are hacking into the secret files of your hated corporations, and military leaders. You love that they are able to outsmart the Powers that Be and take a little back for themselves. You love your computer fantasy games that show you have more skill than the next guy. You love it when you or your heroes do it; but I just happened to do it to a much larger computer and now I'm the bad guy. I figured out how to break Merlin's Matrix code and reinsert my code and hook you all into it and now I'm the bad guy. I believe that I'm the better player. I think that fact is proven by where you all stand right now.

I have put into place leaders that control every country and most of your states. I have created a Military-Industrial complex that answers to me. I have weakened every one of you over and over. I own the weapons. I am the obvious winner in the Game. All you can do at this point is to capitulate to me. I have armies throughout the universe that answer to me. The Nazis are an expression of my reptilian army that has merely morphed into a modern day human consciousness. May the best among you live and prosper and the useless among you become extinct.

Let me tell you something: We play fair. We always announce our intentions. We tell you what we are planning and you are too stupid to respond, interpret or understand. Only a few of you have begun to decode the secret symbols, texts, and images that have been right in front of your faces for thousands of years. I co-opted your sacred symbols and used them for myself. Those of you who do break the codes are often called insane and conspiracy theorists. The Washington Monument stands in tribute to my impalement stakes, in case you wondered. Once again, the ancient symbols are reprogrammed so that they might be utilized by the Family of Dark. The original obelisks, which come from Egypt, stood for the Sun

God, but have been reprogrammed by my family to stand as a tribute to my impalement stakes.

You might ask yourselves why the Family of Dark is so big a family, so brilliant a family, and so much more awake than the Family of Light, who lives in a La La Land prison that they are frightened to venture out of. "Oh, I don't read the news. I don't watch television. Oh, I'm so much more spiritual than you are." You even compete with one another to see who holds the most asleep position as if it is some trophy to be shown. I'm more ignorant and fearful than you and that makes me better than you. I have to say I am most proud of that handy work. Making the Family of Light a bunch of fear-based, groveling, head-in-the-sand idiots has been rather delightful. And watching you turn on one another has been the most fun of all.

I can hear you all now, "Oh, how terrible that Margaret allowed these words to be said about us. She must be a terrible person." I will delight at your judgment of her and these words. For although you all claim to be above judgment you are the most judgmental of all. Here you go again, defending your precious purity against the impure. There you go again, casting dispersions left and right in the name of God.

These are all the things that have led to my success. You all led me there, for if you were all as snowy clean as you claim to be there would have been nothing for me to get ahold of. I needed your weakness to turn you against one another—I used your own failings to destroy you. I didn't need to create more, you all had plenty of them for me to use. Were you able to "Love your Neighbor as Yourself?" Hardly. Even that one has proven difficult for all of you.

Victory itself is my defense. You have been so easy to destroy because you destroyed yourselves with your base, ignorant, stupid, and fearful natures.

MERLIN: MORE ON THE NEPHILIM

I would ask you all to question who has who in checkmate.

As you have been told, Vlad Dracula came to recapture the Earth for himself for he believes that it belongs to both him and his reptilian creations. He believes he was unfairly removed from the Earth and he is only claiming what is rightly his. The dinosaurs have evolved over millions of years, and as you have been shown, the reptilian DNA mutations are widespread throughout the universe. As you now realize, everyone springs from the original Dragon Race. The dragons were the very first creation into density. The fallen angels of the ancient biblical book of Enoch who came to the Earth are the Andromedan officers, the Pleiadian reptilian hybrids, the Annunaki hybrids and the Red and Black Dragons. These beings came to the Earth in what the prophet Ezekiel calls "Wheels with Burning Eyes of Fire." Or as you know them; spaceships.

In the book of Enoch it is told to you that the fallen angels came to the Earth and mated with humans and created the Nephilim. The ET's or fallen angels were reported to be giants and taught humanity many things, including the making of weapons, metal work, how to read the signs of the zodiac and how to anoint themselves with oil and perfumes. They also brought what you know of today as black magic, which is using metaphysical principles to move matter to ones' will, but for selfish or devious purposes. Because this information is so upsetting to most human beings' sense of reality, they have not included Enoch in most of the biblical texts. But, all biblical scholars are familiar with it.

Vlad has managed to fool many people into thinking that if someone has metaphysical knowledge they must be a Lightworker, and be working for good. That is part of the computer program which has been inserted into your consciousness to fall prey to the false prophets. The same goes for organized religion. Many innocents think that if someone stands before them, and can preach, they must be working for good. Even after they are robbed of thousands of dollars they will still fall prey to these preachers.

The same has been true of political figures and other figures of authority. If they hold a position of authority you are taught since childhood that they must know something very important and you should obey and follow their lead. You are beginning to wake up to this charade and realize that those who grab at power do not have your best interests at heart.

The purpose of this reptilian mating was to spread the reptilian DNA to the Earth and once again, just as Vlad did elsewhere, he decided to keep that which seemed useful to him. He realized that humans could be mated with reptilian DNA and used to strengthen his armies. He realized that if he created a human reptilian army they could be used to wipe out my human creation, and finally accomplish his goal. His own reptilian mutations on the Earth could go to war against my human template creations. That is why he allowed the mating to occur and made sure that the new reptilian children were shown how to work with metal to create weapons and how to read signs, symbols and astrology. All of those were "ET" gifts.

Even today the ancient history is evident in those who have Rh negative bloodlines. The Rh refers to Rhesus monkey and those who are Rh negative do not have the human "monkey" template blood—their blood is an expression of the reptilian bloodline. This is also true of what are called the "blue bloods."

It became clear to Vlad that these human reptilians needed to be controlled, or they would begin to come into their own power, and even challenge his own armies. He needed them to be programmed to destroy the "innocent ones on Earth," and reclaim their right to rule. It didn't seem enough to divide the human brain into two lobes; or unplug the DNA strands, Vlad realized that he could use the frequency generating devices he had seen elsewhere in the universe to "dumb down" the human frequency field and even alter the Earth itself. Even though most humans no longer remember that the Earth is a living, conscious being, Vlad is well aware of it. It was around this time that the Lower Matrix came into being. Vlad hacked into my original Matrix and inserted codes to hold the human race captive. Human beings are being programmed to be "asleep" and "dumbed down" from the Lower Matrix. After the Lower Matrix, cults of violence began to assert themselves. Humans began the rituals of bloody sacrifice to appease the gods who were actually reptilian overlords. Feminine power became the enemy as the patriarchal bias and the unfeeling nature of the human race grew and grew. Atlantis devolved into an Annunaki and Andromedan reptilian playground and the baser natures of the reptilians combined with the knowledge of the Andromdans and Sirians on the Earth. Unfortunately the Lower Matrix made sure that they used the knowledge for destruction.

The Roman Empire also devolved into one of the most reptilian civilizations as evidenced by the brutality of the bestiality and the cruelty of their entertainment. It is not my human template that laughs at another human being cruelly pulled apart by horses or mauled by a lion. That is the reptilian template. And that is the template you are always struggling against.

VLAD DRACULA: HACKING INTO THE MATRIX

You must wonder why I am allowing this scribe, Margaret, to reveal my secrets. It is because I have won the Game. The Game is almost over and I won. I control the guns, the food supply, the money, and all the resources. You control nothing. You don't even own your homes or the clothes on your back. I could take it from you in the blink of an eye. So, I want you all to know what was done to you before you go down.

The First Nine Matrix or Computer Program Inserts are the following, in no particular order:

1. Religion: Prior to my inserting a religion program there was nothing resembling an organized method of worship that you needed to follow or believe or you would be doomed. The software has been rewritten to move and change with the times, but it has been inserted to keep you all under control. It became clear to me that without some kind of outside supposedly spiritual "fear of God" put into you all, you would not be so easy to control; hence, religion.

2. Political structure: It's pretty much ditto with that. It became clear, that without some semblance of a power structure and hierarchy to rule the masses, and direct them as I intended, I would be unable to retain my control. I selected the bloodlines

that contained my reptilian DNA and made sure they would rise to power. Prince Charles of England recently stated publicly that he is a direct descendant of Vlad the Impaler—or me. This assured that they would be loyal to my wishes.

3. Self-consciousness: The idea of being self-conscious as you know it today is a product of a software program inserted into the Matrix. It was necessary for you to become self-aware for you to become self-loathing. The idea of Narcissus looking at himself endlessly in the mirror of the lake is a perfect example. When you are an animal you have no self-identity. An animal does not worry about what they look like, nor are they concerned about what you look like. They just are. But if humans are to be controlled they need to become self-conscious about their appearance. The first program was inserted to make humans feel ashamed of their appearance. That is the idea of eating the apple from the Garden of Eden and becoming ashamed. Guess who the snake was? Me! (Have you ever questioned the Apple computer logo?)

4. Self-doubt: The self-doubt program is one of my favorites because it can be manipulated in a myriad of ways. How often have you said to someone who is very talented, "Wow! You are brilliant at that," and have them look at you with eyes of self-doubt? That is my doing. If people didn't suffer so much doubt they would know what to do to overthrow me. Hence, the self-doubt program. Nobody knows how brilliant they really are. The ones who say they are brilliant and get famous are not the most talented. This really screws with all of your minds and weakens you.

5. Anti-Creativity: The anti-creativity program is a program designed to tell you all that artists and visionaries are nuts. At best they are "ahead of their time." It was inserted to make sure that the mediocre human minds rise to power, and the visionaries suffer from obscurity. I don't even need to elaborate on that one. It allows me to control the output of who gets famous and who doesn't. When a visionary slips through the cracks they are often murdered by one of my operatives—a

mind control victim. A perfect example of this is John Lennon, Martin Luther King Jr., Gandhi, and John F. Kennedy.

6. Poverty program: It was necessary to insert a poverty program into the Matrix to keep the wealth, and hence the power, in the proper hands. I think it was brilliant that I inserted into the Bible the idea that wealth corrupts the soul, so that everyone got so confused about wealth and spirituality that they left the rich alone to lose their soul to me and didn't try to get back their money. Many spiritual people still suffer from the "wealth is bad" belief, which allows me to centralize the banks in the hands of the greedy. You won't get into heaven with cash in your pocket. Merlin will tell you that money keeps you away from focusing on what's important—spirit. But, I will tell you that is only because my Lower Matrix controls the software of your brain. Money is your enemy. How many good guys have billions? None. They work for me. Did I confuse you? Yes? Good... stay that way...it suits me.

7. Ownership program: I realized that I needed to up the arrogance factor in your brains, so that you felt it was your right to control the Earth's resources and the animal kingdom for your own purposes. That allowed me to weaken Merlin's Earth creations and control them for my purposes. The idea that you are supreme on the Earth, and everything is to be exploited, is my doing. Even though you are my slaves, this program makes you think you are in control.

8. Alone in the universe program: Sorry for laughing, but I never thought I'd pull this one off, and it amazed even me that I was able to do it. With all the evidence right before your eyes in your ancient monuments and the stars in your sky, my software program that says, "you are the most intelligent thing in the universe and no one else is out there," is the hardest piece of software I've ever had to construct. But, I did it brilliantly, and Galileo almost died for busting that software program. Only because he was willing to pretend to support my software program that declared the Earth the center of the universe was he spared.

9. Don't believe anything except what you see program: Love, love, love that program. It is truly one of my most favorite. Gets you all to deny anything that manages to seep through into your "dumbed- down" consciousness that tells you that there is something other than what you see. Man, that one was brilliant. The software is designed to support only your five senses and doubt anything other. It obviously kept you away from Merlin and his band of so-called Enlightened Masters. Oh, I do love that software program!! Written into the program is the Witch-Burning Program, the Inquisition Program and the belief that anyone who does access anything other than the five senses is working for the devil and must suffer a horrible fate.

I'll leave the 10th program for next time as you absorb these works of brilliance on my part.

MERLIN: ESCAPING FROM THE MATRIX

Everything Vlad said about the programs is essentially accurate, but what he doesn't tell you is that your escape from his Matrix is also through your mind. Your mind is the portal to the higher dimensions and all it requires is for you to release your fear of letting go of the imprinted belief systems. This is much harder than it sounds. Are you ready to let go of everything that defines you?

It is important that I reiterate a previously stated idea so that you truly grasp it. Not only have numbers been "hi-jacked" but other symbols besides the Swastika have been as well. The idea of the skull, which obviously holds knowledge, had the crossbones put over it to frighten you away from the portal of your crown chakra. If your mind is the escape, then it stands to reason that he would want you to fear it. The controlling party does not want to you look at the All Seeing Eye of Horus because it is the Eye of the Soul. Through the Eye of the Soul you can see the pathway to your own freedom as it was designed to be; instead they want you to see the All Controlling Eye at the top of the pyramid which graces the back of your dollar bill. The five-pointed star came from Sirius, and had no evil attached, but was inverted and co-opted by the Satanists. Once again they confuse you by putting you in fear of the very symbols and numerology that was designed to set you free. Don't forget that black magic has been used actively on this planet for a long time now, while white magic has been squelched and poo-pooed.

Prying your fingers from the Lower Matrix belief programming is an arduous task. Your ego and self-identity are completely defined by it, and by now you don't know what is real and what is false. The truth is that somewhere deep inside you still lies the Truth—with a capital T. Your truth, and your story, is deeply buried inside of you. Vlad is counting on you not being brave enough to search it out and then speak of it. He is counting on your neighbors who are still plugged into his program turning on you because of Program # 5: the Anti-Creativity and Visionary program. It takes a very brave soul to swim against the tides.

The best method of release from the program is to write down a list of your belief systems and begin to pry your fingers off of them one-by-one. If you are an intellectual who feels comfortable believing that you know everything there is to know because of your higher education, and it makes you uncomfortable to admit that you don't know much of anything, start there. You don't know anything. Nothing. Nada. It's all made up to make you feel better, make you think you are smarter than the average guy, and keep the separation programs growing. Admit that there are many things you don't know and start to unplug from the intellectual program. It is, after all, only another religion and system of beliefs.

If you are a Christian, and completely plugged into the Jesus program, ask yourself who is Jesus to you really? If you are faking it every time you fall to the floor in rapture because your preacher has raised his hand to you, you might want to start with honesty. Did you really feel what you pretended to feel, and does Jesus need such a show of drama to be with you? Only those who don't know how to truly feel their soul connection to spirit need to show everyone else through fainting and false rapture that they are saved. If you really want a personal relationship with Christ then unplug from the organized one and quietly speak one-on-one with your Christed Consciousness.

If you are a politician or constituent and you believe that the two-party system is the way to go, and you are wedded to the Democrats or Republicans, stop feeding the dualities that keep you at war. You are on the same team—Team Earth Human. Act like it. You are both controlled by Vlad's Matrix program and neither political party is free. Ditto for all others around the world.

Unplug from your identity as male, female, rich, poor, pretty, ugly. Unplug it all. This third dimensional reality is a false Matrix put in place to imprison you. End of story. End of your story.

Now, how did you react to the unplugging? Did you delight when it was suggested that others unplug and agree wholeheartedly with that? Did you find yourself saying: "Oh, yeah those Christians should unplug," but balk at unplugging from your own political party, for example?

The next question that might be on your mind is this: So, why did I (Merlin) let it go on? Why didn't I fight back and kick Vlad's ass? Did it have something to do with being more God-like if I don't fight? Being passive is better? No... I did it to show you all that no matter what is thrown at you, they can never truly win. The only place they can win a battle is on the third or fourth dimension, and they are illusionary realms. But the war is already lost to them. Why? Because it goes against the One and Only Truth that can never be destroyed: We are all made from the same stuff. We all come from the same Source and will return to the same Source and nothing they can do will change that fact. Everyone is tied into that program, and it's the only one that is true.

Vlad's fear-based, separation-consciousness Matrix programs feel real, but they aren't. Your fights with the dark energy of Vlad have strengthened you. You even say it yourself, "what doesn't kill me makes me stronger." Vlad trained my army far better than I ever could have. Vlad taught you that no matter what is done to you, you already are saved. Death is not to be feared. Through death you can always return to Light. Indeed there are denser parts of your consciousness that become held in the fourth dimension after death, but eventually those too will return to you and be re-united.

We have time.

VLAD DRACULA:
MATRIX PROGRAM # 10

Fear of death program: That was needed big time, as Merlin has explained, to keep you all around so we (me and my team) could use your bodies to our advantage. A few primitive tribes were able to break through enough to actually cry at birth and rejoice at death, but the European Missionaries who worked for me made sure they had Christianity (and the fear of God and death) beaten into them.

It has been imperative to keep you locked into my Lower Matrix to make sure you believe in its reality and fear leaving its reality. It has been imperative that you believe that this third dimensional realm matters no matter how much suffering it brings to you. That was a tricky one to pull off, because I had to overwhelm the natural impulse inside you to escape pain. I had to connect pleasure with pain and essentially turn you all into masochists, so that you would be willing to endure anything rather than exit the Earth. If you consider this you will indeed come to understand that humans have a huge masochistic streak in them.

The belief that hell exists somewhere else was an essential propaganda tool to keep you all enslaved. I do find it rather humorous that, although the Earth is filled with starvation, pain, torture and fear you believe that there is something worse somewhere else. Everything you fear is right on Earth. This is the hell realm and you are hooked into it as long as you believe in my Lower Matrix programs, which I assure you that you will, until I release you.

Fear of death was an essential program to play the Game.

MERLIN:
THE EXPANSION OF CREATION

When separation was first created by the fall into density, the battle wasn't as fierce as it is today. Originally you might say it was more like a scuffle. As individual identification grew, so did disagreements. The best way to describe the situation, so that a human mind can perceive it, is to talk about this stage like a human toddler stage. The toddler, in her growing self-awareness, begins to demand things for herself. She begins to want this and that and often refuses to share. This is similar to what happened with the dragons. Once they could materialize energy into form it became possible for the dragons to own things that they had created, things that set them apart—things that others hadn't created. In the higher dimensional realms, since pure consciousness decides what you get, and what you don't get, you don't want what you can't imagine for yourself in heaven.

Once density set in, and you could actually desire something that someone else had created, the dragons became contentious and even thieving. They still had the power of thinking things into creation, and they could materialize with thought, because they were still very fourth dimensional. Their bodies shimmered between what you would think of as fourth and third dimension. Because the fourth dimension is a highly mutable dimension, which responds instantly to consciousness, they could still think and instantly manifest their reality. Their bodies and creations would appear to you today to be almost shimmering illusions, like ghosts, who could come into density and then disappear and reappear. Arguments sprang up as their bodies hardened and fear took over. Fear was a new emotion manifested from the separation consciousness they had begun to express. Fear spreads rapidly when it becomes a motivating force for behavior. Suddenly many of the dragon/angels felt lost and angry, and thoughts of revenge filled their minds as they began to imagine destroying the heaven realm and becoming the victors by bringing down all the angels.

Time is meaningless in these realms. Millions of years seem like a blink. Creation at this level is not measured by time as you know it. Nor is it measured by distance as you know it. Again, I must reiterate that Vlad's Lower Matrix keeps you tethered so you can be controlled. The Time and Space Program he inserted is a part of the enslavement package he has presented to all of you. I'm sure he will be happy to talk about those programs shortly.

One of the earliest settlements of the dragons was in the multiple star system of Lyra, and it was the home of the White Dragons, Rainbow Dragons and later the Dragons of the Noble Heart. As I mentioned the Dragons of the Noble heart are a group of dragons who have joined in service to me to battle Vlad Dracula's rule. Lyra contains many of the Ancient Ones who wanted to get away from the chaos and dark abode of Orion. These dragons wanted to start a world that would be more peaceful and less contentious. They were some of the earliest beings to attempt to organize a world that wasn't just a prison of chaos and control, such as grew to exist in Orion.

Out of the multiple star system of Lyra came many of the other life forms that populate the universe, because it's where the Seeker School began. In many ways you could say it's where the original Seekers, or Life Creators, got their start. As creation in the fourth, and even the third dimension seemed to be in full swing, it was decided by the upper realms of Angelic Beings that if this was the direction the universe was taking, then some of us had better be trained in life creation, otherwise the Orion dragons were going to be free to manifest hell realm after hell realm with no other forces balancing their energy.

I emerged as a Creator God quite early because I had been somewhat successful at bridging the gap between the fallen angels and the angels of the upper realms, and so was in charge of compiling a group of beings that I felt had the gifts and temperament to begin consciously creating life, and organizing and seeding the galaxies with their creations. I had been able to bridge the realms because early on I had been willing to reach down to the fallen angels and communicate with them. I brought back the information to the upper realms that fighting was breaking out among the fallen angel-dragons. Fighting, as you can imagine, was a very new concept to those still ensconced in heaven. It was because I was trying to bridge this gap that I chose Vlad Dracula to be a student of mine. I felt that if I could tutor him, and help him to learn life creation with respect and balance, it would do much to bring balance to the universe. It was for that reason I extended a hand to Vlad Dracula—a most impressive dragon—and invited him to join me and my newly formed band of students. Vlad had already emerged as a leader in Orion, and I felt that if I could get him to work with me, I stood a chance to put an end to the chaos coming out of his star system.

Lyra was where we began our work, and many of the first and most original templates began to emerge. The feline template is an ancient one that originates in Lyra, for example. Man and woman as you know it had not yet been conceived. Biological forms also began to emerge as my life creators began to conceive of color and shape and learn the methods of balancing the energies of creation; what you call yin and yang. This is using opposing forces to bring tension to matter and create life. In the earliest years the work was always intensely joyful. Imagine your most joyful moment of creational bliss, then magnify that times thousands. Creator Gods organized galaxies, created planets and began the exciting work of populating the third, fourth, fifth and other dimensions.

Being in a state of creation is the closest we can come to the orgasmic ecstasy that God feels as She explodes into creational energy and matter. It all comes from a powerful sneeze, belch or orgasm of creational joy. When you create you are God-like.

VLAD DRACULA: THE TIME AND SPACE MATRIX PROGRAMS

From the very beginning I knew that in order to lock my captured beings into prison, it became quite evident to me that they needed to be locked into time and space programs that would serve as prison bars. I realized that to create the perfect prison I needed to separate time and space. In truth time is "spacial," but by separating time and space I could lock my prisoners into jail just as if I had iron bars and a key.

I realized that if I restricted humans from accessing information, or moving through time and space, then I made them prisoners of their meaningless life experiences. I marvel at how humans, stuck in their narrow consciousness, still try to attach meaning to their life. It's pretty pitiful actually. I gloat over that quite a bit. Humans try to make assumptions and understandings in such limited ways by drawing on maybe twenty, thirty, forty or fifty years of experiences in one lifetime. Then they try to sound wise, and convince themselves that they know what to do, and what to tell others to do. Most humans know they don't really know what the hell they are doing, but if they can convince you that they know something, maybe they can convince themselves. It really is a case of "the blind leading the blind."

Separating time from space would not have been possible without the disconnection and alteration of the human body, and so it required disconnecting your DNA and splitting your brain into two lobes. If your right brain and left brain do not work together, then your right brain (which remembers the feeling of expansion and will release you from time and space restrictions) cannot properly link up to your left brain (which gives you the ability to understand and analyze your experiences more logically) and you cannot truly remember how to be multi-dimensional, and use the other dimensions to break the time/space barrier. The "junk DNA," as it is called, is the DNA that awakens what you humans would call your upper chakras, or the ones off the body.

Until the crown chakra can be informed by chakras that plug directly into galactic consciousness, you are restricted to accessing information that is in your immediate environment. Only those who can sustain the awakening of the crown chakra, and then connect it to the most subtle chakras 'off-body,' even stand a chance of receiving information from outside the Earth. The Galactic Chakra system was shut-off when the DNA was unplugged.

TELEPATHIC COMMUNCATION UNPLUG

Humans were originally designed by Merlin to be telepathic communicators. It was his belief that if you could not hide your thoughts you could not live in separation and work against one another. As a result it became very evident to me, quite early on, that telepathic communication was my enemy and had to be dealt with. I knew that the Time and Space Matrix would destroy most people's ability to be telepathic because of the alterations to the human body. I also depended on the other Matrix programs such as the Anti-Visionary Program to squelch those who were able to rise above the five senses and begin to read minds.

As the mind control experiments on the Earth evolved, I watched over the scientists' work making sure that the experiments were used for Matrix control, not Matrix release. Scientists are even able to enter people during their dream states—they plug into the Matrix a dream which is fed into the receptive fourth dimensional brain during sleep. That way I can download into you while you are sleeping whatever I want you to manifest while you are awake.

This keeps you all in fear, and is exactly what I need to finish you all off. I'm sorry to be the bearer of bad news, but you guys don't stand a chance.

MERLIN: WHAT ARE YOU GOING TO DO ABOUT IT?

Okay. You've heard what he did to you. Now what are you going to do about it? Are you going to continue to live disconnected, fear-based, angry lives? Are you going to buy into Vlad's programs and let him win? That is the question you must ask yourself now, for what he doesn't tell you, once again, is that you can get free. Do you want to love people and join in with them, or do you want to pout, continue to get angry at people at the drop of a hat by being triggered and exploding at every minute? Even if you have been programmed to do the negative behaviors you can override these behaviors with greater awareness. Do you want to pull away from people, and tell yourself that you hate them, or do you want to love and help them? Vlad is giving you the opportunity to choose, and by choosing he is giving you the opportunity to "know thyself." Without Vlad you would not have the push and pull of dark and light which allows you to know where it is you stand in the equation. Without Vlad you would have no choice.

So, isn't it interesting that your jailer is also giving you an opportunity for divine choice? Vlad gives you something even as he takes it away from you. Vlad lets you choose between your dark fear-based nature, and your light fearless nature.

If Vlad is a mirror for your own darkness, what do you choose? All the beings of Light know that choosing the Light will serve you far more than any other choice you could make.

BREAKING VLAD'S LOWER MATRIX

Key to breaking the Lower Matrix is the idea that your behavior is aligned with your thoughts and words. Because action has powerful energy that moves matter instantly, it is important that you match all three of these things. Most of you are strong in one or maybe two of these areas—thoughts and words, or words and action. But you are not aligned in all three. It might surprise you to find out that many people who act like they are nice people are actually quite plagued by dark thoughts. And many people who find it easy to align their thoughts and words with Higher Truth cannot follow through with their actions. In order to break free from the Lower Matrix, and not feed it, it is important to be able to be consistent in your life. This is the most difficult task you face.

The most important thing to consistency is self-awareness. How many of you really know what you are thinking or are even aware of the impact of your words? You tell yourself that it doesn't matter that you say something mean to yourself or someone else—as long as you pretend in your actions to be nice to them, for example. You cannot be a different person everywhere you go. You must be the same person, an integrated person, everywhere and with everyone.

It was mentioned that during sleep you can be vulnerable to the computer Matrix programs that Vlad wants you to receive, and that many of you having the same dream at night are picking up on the same computer download. Raising your frequency with integration of your energetic fields, and utilizing techniques to keep your vibration lifted while moving in and out of body during sleep, will also assist you to break free from the Lower Matrix. If you go to bed with the television on, you are asking for negatively programmed downloads to enter your consciousness. If you are watching violent television before bed, then you are ripe for violent downloading. There is a reason that most television programs today are either vapid or violent. The vapid ones keep you focused on the material and unimportant trivia to divert you from what's really going on, and the violent ones keep your reptilian brain activated so that you are more easily programmed and will help Vlad's chaos programming.

You are held within some very dark energy on the Earth. Now that you know it what will you do? Will you support this energy with your thoughts, words and actions? Or will you break free from dark energy with your thoughts, words and actions? The choice is ultimately yours no matter what Vlad does to you.

VLAD DRACULA: I AM THE DRAGON GOD

It is important to me that you all understand that Jesus and I are very similar; and that you learn that it is me who you must worship, and not Jesus. You will be given an opportunity in the near future to see the truth of who your savior really is, me. You have been falsely led astray by the Merlin consciousness to believe in your superiority. You have been falsely led to believe that you are powerful and in control, and it should be quite obvious by now (or will be to all of you shortly) that you are anything but in control. Everyone you have trusted has lied to you.

That is important for you to experience, so that you turn to me for truth. Your false prophets are everywhere preaching Jesus, and then having sex with children and snorting cocaine or stealing your money. Can you still trust them? Jesus has led you astray, and those who told you that the Bible was the word of God have lied to you. How many false prophets have appeared recently? I wrote the Book of Revelations. Sit with that. I knew what the End of Days would hold for all of you: Me.

I am the one who doesn't lie to you. I tell you straight up what's going on, and what I believe and what will happen to you. You are going to shift from worshipping Jesus to worshipping the true leader of this universe. I am the Son of Dragon and the rightful ruler of the worlds.

Jesus is a knock-off, liar, who conned you all into believing something that didn't exist. Soon enough you will know your true boss. Religion was my program, because I wasn't ready to reveal myself, and I wanted you all to understand the lies that were being heaped on you by Merlin. I set up the religion programs to keep you in the dark, and confused until I was ready to reveal myself to you, and reveal the truth to you. You needed the knowledge of the lies to finally see Truth.

I have been around longer than anyone. My people, the dragons and the reptilians, are the true owners of the universe. In me is the template you are to revere. Jesus is a bad Merlin knock-off sent down to make you think you have power you don't have. You keep hearing that you can change water into wine like Jesus, but have any of you accomplished that yet? No. Why? Because it's a lie. You have no real power because Merlin's creation is inferior to my creation. Why? Because my creation is the original template which came down from heaven and Merlin's creation, Man and Woman, came from him and not from heaven.

You've been duped, but I'm not the one duping you. He is.

MERLIN: THE TEMPLATE WAR

Okay, so now it's clear to all of you that you are in the midst of a template war between the Dracula reptilians, and the Merlin humans. I will tell you that reptilians are cold-hearted, as well as cold-blooded. They do not have the ability to feel compassion like you do. They do not have the ability to feel love like you do. They feed their own interests. If you behave like that then you are serving them. If you serve others with compassion, you are serving love. What is it you choose to serve?

The energy of the divine feminine and the divine masculine was originally designed to balance one another and create a situation of harmonious tension—opposites attract was the idea. Although you live in a patriarchal society, it might surprise you to know that there have been matriarchal societies on the Earth as well. So, before we get too masculine in this history lesson it's time to bring in the divine feminine aspects and the counter-punch of the patriarchy.

The original expression of sexuality, as I designed it, was the perfect expression of the system of outside regulation (as I discussed earlier). In order for beings to need each other, I designed this concept of using other beings outside of oneself to serve as "mirrors" and "strengths." That meant that each individual being would not need to do everything alone, and I had hoped it would foster an interdependence that would draw you all closer to one another. If you needed each other to survive, I surmised, then you would work together. Men and women could not survive without one another; what better way to make sure they worked together. Or so I thought.

Childbirth was designed as a joyful occasion, meant to be an orgasm of birth as the portal to the divine realms opened, and an angelic piece of creation was brought down to the Earth. But, divide and conquer has been Vlad's method of operation for a long time. He knew that I had designed this system of balance, and figured if he could create duality that would lead to war instead of peace (as I had envisioned), then humans would fight against one another while he rested. He knew once he got you all stirred up then you would kill each other for him. But in order to achieve this warring at each other, instead of depending on each other for your survival, he had to make one sex stronger than the other. Dividing the brain into two lobes—yin and yang—made this duality possible.

His first choice was to make the feminine stronger because as he has told you he prefers women to men overall. He understood that women had something inherently fierce about them due to one thing—I had designed women to bond to their offspring powerfully in order to protect them. It was this fierceness that attracted him. Men, he surmised, could be taught to fight due to their superior physical strength, but women could be manipulated emotionally. So, his first intention was to seduce women and whisper in their ears about the inferiority of men. He wanted to turn them against men, and teach them to dominate men, and use them as mere breeding stock. That way, he figured, my creation would be out of balance and soon they would fight one another. Once the momentum had been set in motion he could sit back and watch the fight.

Women grew very powerful, and eventually the temple priestess culture devolved so much that many of these women enslaved men, and used them for physical labor and physical pleasure, with no regard to what the man's own needs were. Men were considered stupid; too stupid to actually rule and make laws and set agendas. Women grew drunk with their own power and began to fight one another. They became masters at secret agendas and double crossing. But whenever anything falls out of balance, chaos ensues, and the scales must be righted. So, men revolted. They began to physically dominate and enslave women and "take back their power," in violent ways. The see-saw of sexuality was about to tip toward the patriarchy, and the battle between the sexes was in full swing.

As you are now beginning to understand the reptilians are interbred throughout the universe and many humans on the Earth have reptilian DNA/blood as well. So, although there are the Annunaki reptilians from the Sirian star system, Pleiadian reptilians from the Pleiades, Andromedan reptilians and the Grays taken from the rejected Arcturians at the time of quarantine on Arcturus, there are also those who were created directly from stolen humans. One of these groups is the Antareans from Antares star system. These beings are hybrids from the human reptilian template designed to serve as military leaders on Earth.

Vlad Dracula wanted a species that would be strong enough to overwhelm the majority of human beings both energetically and physically, and again it was an experiment to create a mixed species that genetically suited him. He tinkered with the human template and created the Antareans. But, like all other hybrid mixes, the Antareans have infiltrated the human experience so profoundly by now that they are quite connected, and interested in what goes on here. They were bred to rule the Earth's armies, after all.

These traits of arrogance and domination were bred into them from the reptilian template. In this case Vlad wanted to see if he could create a human reptilian army that would serve his needs, and become his Earth generals. These beings most often show up in elevated military positions, and serve the armies of the Earth. It suits Vlad's plan to keep the chaos and fear going on the Earth to keep humans away from their divine, peaceful selves, so he created these beings to make sure a military/industrial complex would do his bidding in this way. They vary slightly from the Annunaki/reptilian world leaders in that they have a gruffness and crudeness about them that the Annunaki world leaders often do not have.   —TRUMP

The Antareans have molded themselves into armies of organized crime as well, and the Mafia is riddled with beings from Antares. These are an expression of Vlad's reptilian-human, super race. Because they are human-based, these beings are very human, and it is in part why the human race is thought to be a violent species. The original human template was not a violent one, but the experimentation and re-seeding with the beings from the Antares/hybrid strain made sure that the violent tendencies would continue to feed the military rulers. Often, for example, the King would be Annunaki, but his general would be from Antares.

Every government on the Earth at this time, that has any power whatsoever, has an army that is intimately connected to the political rulers. In America the CIA and the military believe themselves to be superior to the President and his staff, and they rule behind the scenes. They have a public face and a private face. The private face is the Antarean general willing to take orders from no one. What you call dictatorships are often the wedding of the Antarean military leader, with the presidential position, to rule directly.

In ancient times these Titans who ruled the world were the Greek and Roman Gods. They appeared human in their build, but they were superior to humans. That is why Zeus was depicted as throwing lightning bolts. It is also why Zeus loved to mate with many different beings—a reptilian trait to be sure. Not all the gods were evil, but all the gods thought themselves superior to mere mortals, because they were an expression of the Overlords' idealized creation. They were human hybrids.

The Titans are not an original template, meaning that they were a co-opted hybrid creation, and were not a Creator God's original template. Vlad's army stole humans from the Earth and brought them to Antares to perfect them as rulers of the Earth by blending traits from many different enslaved species. From there he created the Titans or gods who were sent to rule and control the Earth. The Titans are essentially a created species from many different species. It is because of this that they rule the Ocean, the Heavens, the Earth, and almost every facet of creation in mythology. It was more or less Vlad's attempt to make superhuman rulers. In your modern mythology you have Superman—a super human who comes from Krypton, a planet that revolves around Antares.

The Titans were considered the elite among the Antareans, and Mars was originally a colony that was established for Earth's ruling elite. It was a place that they could meet to plan their next strategy and it was often visited by Annunaki, Antareans and Titans as well as reptilian soldiers and the Andromedan generals. It was a meeting place for those who considered themselves Rulers of the Universe. Because of that it became a target of attack. The attack was done by infiltration. The Galactic Federation of Light and the Council of War sent in double agents to infiltrate the elite of Mars. A large meeting, which brought everyone together, was arranged, and the Galactic Federation attacked in an attempt to destroy the leaders of Vlad's reptilian army. The fighting was fierce. The battle destroyed Mars' surface, making the once life-filled surface uninhabitable.

VLAD DRACULA: CREATION OF THE TITANS *and* ANTAREANS

The Titans are my way of thumbing my nose at Merlin. I took his human template and made superior beings. I wanted to show him that I could take his original human creation and actually perfect it. You call them superheroes or gods, but I call them a fun experiment. I figured that if I could make larger than life humans, and show Merlin how wimpy his creation looked next to mine, I could prove my superiority to him. And if I could get Merlin's humans to look up to my superheroes and worship them, even better.

I created the Antarean-reptilian blend in collaboration with a Creator God who had agreed to work with me. He thought it might bring me back into the fold; back to the table. What a fool! Even Merlin warned him against this collaboration, but he wouldn't listen to Merlin. He felt that if he could win me back, to sit with the Council of Creator Gods in collaborative harmony, then he would be doing a "good" thing. So, he stated a condition, and that was that he could retain some measure of control over the creation; as if he could set conditions with me! I agreed because I knew that in the end I would have control over the entire universe. So what did it matter what I agreed to? I wanted his help for one reason only: I'd seen what he had done with another species, and liked his results.

The species I was enamored of had the ability to grow larger or smaller, and they also had the ability to camouflage themselves at will.

They appear as huge snake-like creatures, but can also reduce their size into small shrunken bodies, and blend into the surroundings. Their bodies will mimic the surroundings until they attack. When they seize their prey the camouflage is dropped and they grow to their full width and length. There is not a human name for them as they are unknown to earthlings. I call them "Greblacks."

This DNA merge allowed me to develop the camouflage for the reptilian human. I knew reptilian camouflage would be necessary for the new species to blend into the human race. I needed the Greblack DNA to make a human reptilian that could move successfully between human and reptilian. Unfortunately, the human reptilian shapeshifters (who are bred from this stock) often find themselves fighting to maintain control of their shapeshifting abilities. As a result human emotion can sometimes get the best of them, and they will shift partially or permanently without full control over the experience. When you think of a reptilian shapeshifter most of you think of a "monster-type" of being. The Incredible Hulk cartoon is based on some of those ideas.

Many human reptilian shapeshifters will choose to be loners as they realize that their "secret" might be found out. Many human hybrids also stick together because it is more comfortable. It is my great joy to let them know that there will come a day soon enough when they can come out of hiding altogether.

MERLIN: ROBOTS AND THEIR INFLUENCE ON EARTH

The robots have been working throughout the universe, and on the Earth, for a long time. On the Earth you will see them depicted on ancient monuments, which should indicate to you that their influence is not just modern. Where do these robotic beings come from? Does Vlad control them? Do they have free will? Are they good or evil?

These inorganic beings have been used for millions of years to conquer and invade. Their agenda is aligned with the agendas of the other invasive extra-terrestrial species such as the reptilians. Essentially they are working toward the same end which is Vlad's end: Conquer or destroy human DNA, capture the human soul, re-create the human soul, study the human soul template, and so forth.

What most people think of as "the robots" were developed hundreds of thousands of years ago after the Andromendan invasion—or perhaps it is best to say the Andromedan persuasion—as Vlad persuaded many of the Andromedan scientists to work with him. Some call them Ancrans, other Archons. They were created by Andromedan scientists to assist Vlad Dracula's army. Andromedans love perfected systems, as has been explained to you, so it wasn't hard to convince an Andromedan scientist to work on a perfected system like a robot. Many of the leaders of the computer industry on the Earth are the reincarnation of the Andromedan scientists, and worked with Vlad Dracula many thousands of years ago. They are addicted to perfected systems and thought, and have a tendency to be very impatient with those who are imperfect. Unfortunately, when their egos get stimulated they are easily persuaded to manifest their dark side.

It became clear to Vlad that he wanted to develop beings that could be programmed to respond to his every desire and would have no other will but to serve. Although his reptilian soldiers were loyal to him, they were anything but simple to control, since they were able to feel many of the baser emotions such as anger and revenge. Vlad knew that he needed a less biological life form, and the Andromedan scientists seemed just the ones to deliver his vision and make it real for him. As these robots have developed from unensouled machines, to far more sophisticated creations, the neo-Nazi scientists on the Earth have been working to perfect the idea of combining a soul from a human with a robot, and still maintaining control of the system.

Today Vlad's robot army is quite sophisticated, but originally robots were designed to pilot the ships, repair the ships, navigate, and so forth. Later they became an integral part of maintaining Vlad's Lower Matrix on Earth—and those who have been contacted by them understand this. The famous (or infamous) MIB's (Men in Black) are expressions of the Archon robots. These beings were depicted in the movie *Matrix* as Agent Smith. They serve without emotion and go where they are sent. Many humans have had interactions with them and will attest that they are indeed real and very frightening.

In the beginning the robots seemed to be a perfect solution to designing and assembling an army to begin his inter-galactic conquest. The issue of an individual's will asserting itself would not interfere in his plans, and he could count on them to do what needed to be done without fear. They are truly fearless. Since they would be unensouled, Vlad figured they would have no fear of death, or of killing when necessary. It seemed to him that these beings were going to fulfill a very prominent gap in his army up to that point.

As all things have evolved, so too have the robotic beings. Currently the mainstream media is being deluded to make you believe that these robot creations are, for the first time, being perfected to look human; but they are, in truth, all around you and have been for some time. For those of you interested in historical references, you will find that the Greek God Hephaestus (who was also known as Vulcan in the Roman tradition—a Vulcan is an Andromedan) was credited with creating robotic beings, and Chinese accounts relate a history of robots back to the 10th century BC when Yan Shi is credited with making an automaton resembling a human. Once again you have been fooled to believe that the idea of robots is a modern one.

Ultimately Vlad wishes to perfect the robotic creation so that he can turn all of my human beings into his half human/half robot slaves. This is why the neo-Nazi scientists are working to steal souls, corrupt those souls by altering their composition, and then re-implant them into human robot clones. Their plan is this: The elite rulers will be non-robots, but the slaves will be human/robot clones. If you need a job done, what better agent than a human/robot to do it for you? The pure robots are unable to fool the typical human into believing they were real, but these human/robot clones are far more effective.

The original robot army that Vlad created assists him with such tasks as programming and re-programming, and defending the Lower Matrix. Robots are used for many purposes, and most humans holding a tremendous position of power will have a robot constructed of them to serve as a double. In that way Vlad can control the human completely, especially when they are giving public appearances. I'm sure you can all think of a situation where you believed that the individual you witnessed on television was a robot.

Vlad's biggest concern is the problem of the robots becoming self-aware. Once a being is self-aware the issue of how to control them becomes extremely complex. There is a fine line between self-aware and self-knowledge, and it is difficult to build into a robot's computer function the ability to be self-aware enough to appear lifelike, but not so much that they suddenly have a consciousness separate from the control system.

Ideally the software and computer program will not mutate, but at the level of sophistication that Vlad is dealing—especially as his scientists are now perfecting the idea of inserting a human soul into the robot—he and his scientists cannot be 100% in control. They have done many experiments where a robot clone will appear to "short circuit" and get lost or confused. If a robot clone is designed for a simple function, such as to answer questions in a pre-arranged press conference, there is no need for complex self-aware systems to be designed. But, if a robotic being must interact in a myriad of situations which are uncontrollable, then the control systems are challenged. You have to create a program which allows the being to make decisions for themselves, as you cannot program every experience possibility into a robot. As a result the robots have the potential to mutate and think for themselves in all matters. That includes morality. This is where Vlad's Nazi scientists are getting held up in their experiment. As they design and re-design these beings they encounter a myriad of problems.

The unensouled robots are without feeling, and they can be more brutal than even the reptilian soldiers due to the fact that they have absolutely no biological components. They will do exactly what they are programmed to do. There is no internal fight between a soul and a computer. There is no fight or flight; there is only fight. They have no awareness of "God" or anything other than what they are programmed to know. But, as I mentioned that is limited by the program itself. As scientists work in their underground laboratories to perfect these beings you may notice more and more people around you don't seem "quite human."

VLAD DRACULA: THE WAR ON MARS

The war on Mars taught me to keep a closer eye on my military generals, and don't allow them to make decisions independently. I thought I could delegate responsibility to my generals and military leaders, but in the end I overlooked the traitor who was amongst my ranks. I wasn't being diligent enough. Since then each and every time a meeting of upper level generals on the Earth takes place, a DNA scan is done to assure everyone in the room that the attendees are who they say they are. That way one of Merlin's army cannot sneak into my ranks.

After the war on Mars I made sure that every reptilian general would contain the Greblack/Antearan DNA necessary to disguise themselves—if they do not have the ability to disguise, or shapeshift at will, they are not a member of my inner circle. Every top leader who is involved in world domination "behind the scenes" must be capable of shapeshifting at will; that assures the others that they are among their own kind. There are no Archon robots involved at the very highest levels of decision making. The Archons carry out orders; they do not dictate them. Every person at the table has been seen to shapeshift by every other person, for not only does that assure them that all the others have reptilian blood, but it keeps the secrets safe. The leaders of the world who are not able to shapeshift are mistrusted and never allowed in at the most secret meetings. These are the beings who are the "face" of leadership but have no real power behind the throne. These beings are often sacrificed—used and then killed when the time is right and I need an Antarean to take over.

A perfect example of this is John F. Kennedy and Lyndon Baines Johnson. Lyndon is an Antarean general and was needed to escalate and control the Vietnam War, and put money in the pockets of the world's true handlers; something which Kennedy was unwilling to do. Kennedy's attempt to break the United States away from the bank of the Federal Reserve let all of us know that he was now uncontrollable and had to be eliminated. Although he had come from a reptilian line, he was not a true shapeshifter.

It is thought by many humans that every reptilian contains the ability to shapeshift merely because they have some reptilian blood or DNA, and this is not true. The shapeshifters are a special breed of reptilian and they utilize this gift as a means to integrate themselves in to human society and control human populations from within. The shapeshifters have DNA from this Greblack line—they are the reptilian shapeshifters. They may originally be Sirian Annuanki but what allows them to shapeshift is the DNA from the reptilian hybrid line that has been interbred with them.

At this time there are humans who have reptilian blood but it is so diluted that it is useless to me, and to them. They may come from a lineage of reptilians but it has long since become so diluted that they are more human than dragon or dinosaur. Having Rh negative blood does not mean you are a reptilian shapeshifter. It merely means that long ago someone in your ancestry came from my line, and how you express the traits is up to you. I do not care about someone merely because they have Rh negative blood! It is not enough to assure you a position of power within my regime!

There are those who have attempted to blend reptilian DNA into their bodies in order to infiltrate my inner circle. Some have succeeded for a short while; however, the very traits that are carried in the DNA itself make it quite difficult for such an individual to resist the pull of being reptilian. Only a very strong will could override successfully the pull of being reptilian, and even if they died and were reincarnated, they would still find it difficult to break the reptilian ties. I will admit that in rare cases it has been done, but it's not common. Some have consciously chosen to undergo a dilution through taking on many different bodies and incarnating in many different forms in the attempt to remove the reptilian from within them. It is somewhat successful, but any contract made with me will be "called in" eventually regardless of how hard the individual attempts to run from it.

THE TRAITORS ON MARS

My generals became too complacent as the Galactic Federation of Light had mounted no serious attacks on our strongholds for so long. The officers believed they had pushed them back and disarmed them and so became lazy. Little did they know that the quiet came about due to a new plan on the part of our enemy; infiltrate the ranks. It was a dangerous plan, and I will give my enemy credit where it's due. It is one of their largest successes. They won that battle but they won't win the war.

The Galactic Federation of Light worked with three traitors. Two of them had military rank and one of them was a lowly errand boy. The idea was that, if the higher ranking officers were discovered, the errand boy would be able to continue unnoticed. As it turned out the errand boy was killed by a particularly brutal Antarean officer who was displeased with his service. He was the one who was killed and rendered useless. When he was killed, the Galactic Federation was completely dependent on the two officers. One of them was posed as an Andromedan/reptilian scientist although he was loyal to the Andromedean opposition, and the other one was an elevated-rank Annunaki, who defected when he discovered that he was never going to be promoted, and sought revenge on his superiors. It was their idea to hold a meeting that would bring together many of the highest ranking members of my army to share information and plans for sealing the Earth's conquest.

For a long time the reptilian-based army had been in control, and as a result of this they became complacent. A call went out that a meeting of the Family of Dark Alliance was gathering. Security systems were lax and left the members open to attack. Mars was one of the few places I suffered a great loss.

But, just as I did in my life on the Earth as Vlad the Impaler,

I learn from my mistakes at war. Many of the more powerful Lightworkers on the Earth have been infiltrated by members of the Family of Dark in much the same way as I was infiltrated on Mars. Send in people posing as Family of Light, gain the trust, and dismantle the operation from the inside. My enemies do not get off easily.

MERLIN: STONEHENGE AND VLAD DRACULA

Stonehenge was built at the site of the portal of my final battle with Vlad Dracula before I sent him away to Alpha Draconis. It was a pitched battle, and if your mind is reeling with images of two Wizards—one white and one dark—throwing energy balls at one another, you are pretty close! In the end I opened a portal to Alpha Draconis on that spot and sent Vlad back through it before shutting it off behind him. The dinosaurs had already been removed, and I needed to rid the Earth of their creator. He wouldn't go peacefully, as you can well imagine.

Stonehenge has been fought over ever since, as have most of the great power points on the Earth. When the dark forces have had control over Stonehenge, it has been used to gather energy as a power source to use over others. Those who could draw lightening from the sky would energize the stones and the portal itself by infusing the stones with electricity. It would serve as an electric fence to block those with lesser powers from entering or using the portal for their own means. Sometimes those who wanted to control the portal would bury themselves there, sacrifice others there, and commit murder there. It was understood that the trapped souls would serve as ghosts guarding the portal for their masters.

Humans realized that the structure had powerful and strange energies attached to it and have been drawn to it for thousands of years. The structure has been dismantled with age, but the portal remains.

Every wizard who has worked in Stonehenge has wanted to capture my energy that still resides there and use it for their own purposes. They know that I left a large part of myself in that very location, guarding the portal and maintaining its entrance. On the etheric plane of existence my dragons of the Noble Heart stand guard.

Since I closed it behind Vlad it has never been fully re-opened. The spell I cast to keep it closed was a powerful one. Many have tried and have succeeded to lesser and greater degrees. When the time is right it is my intention to realign the portal with Cygnus and utilize it as a gateway to that star system instead.

Stonehenge stands as a monument to our battle and the battle between good and evil. Vlad longs to fully re-open Stonehenge and claim it as his own portal, so that his Black Dragons may re-enter the Earth and manifest in the third dimension once again through it. But, although it has been fought over, he has yet to manage to break the spell I cast upon the spot.

VLAD DRACULA: STONEHENGE THE BATTLE

Merlin gloats over the Stonehenge battle, which is typical of a retired general reliving his glory days. Since our battle in that spot I have opened plenty of portals on the Earth and used them to my advantage. The Betelgeuse portal is only one of the many other portals that serve my needs. Do not flatter yourself, Old Man, into thinking that I care a whit about Stonehenge. Your secrets are useless and old. My army has moved on. Perhaps you might want to try it sometime. You might be more successful against me.

MERLIN: I don't believe that for a moment, and I suggest you don't as well. Vlad cares very much about the Stonehenge portal. Very much.

MERLIN: THE NEANDERTHALS AND THE ET BLOODLINES

The Neanderthals were not my creation. They were created by an advanced student working in my Seeker school under my tutelage. He had created the ape-line and was interested in evolving his species. I gave him permission to do so, and supervised his work as he attempted to blend the ape-like beings with the superior original human template that I had created. He asked me if he could be allowed to evolve some of his apes into a human-like creation. I said, "Yes." I am not so arrogant as to stop an advanced student from working his own line of creation, even if the end product is another type of human. There are many types of human species throughout the universe, and I merely provided the perfected template that they often aspire to re-create or duplicate in their own manner. Each human species has its own specifications which are determined by the planetary constructs they live on and the creational desires of the Creator God.

The reason that the Earth scientists saw such a quick evolutionary jump in the Neanderthal line was because this student *did* use what you all think of as Extra Terrestrial DNA to evolve the species. This means that he drew from my template and elsewhere. When you assume that the only template for a human species is an ape—and you watch only a portion of that species evolve into mankind—then you wonder, "Why not all the ape-like species?" and "Why did those apes develop in a manner that seems different than the rest of the species evolve on Earth?"

If you accept the idea that there is a Creator God School (the Seekers) and you accept that these Creator Gods are responsible for the creation, and subsequently the evolution of their created species, you begin to have a template large enough to encompass what you see around you on the Earth. Many Creator Gods have been working on Earth. That is why there is such a variety of species here.

Was this Creator God an evil reptilian being who inserted his reptilian DNA into the Neanderthal line to make evil humans? In this case the answer is No. The Neanderthal evolution is not a reptilian construct. It is the attempt by a Creator God to evolve his line, blend it with my human template, and be successful with their survival. This is why the brain of the Neanderthals grew so quickly. Once this Creator God decided that he wanted some of his creations to have the ability to solve some of the more sophisticated problems they would encounter, it became necessary to evolve their brains.

My human template was developed to be a template for my students, something to utilize as they created their species. This Creator God was doing just that.

But, you ask, did the reptilian gods, once they had captured the Earth, interfere in manipulating human DNA and this evolutionary line? It should be pretty clear by now that the answer is yes. When the gods began to arrive in space ships and mated with the humans they interfered with this Creator God's vision and the Neanderthals evolved, along with other humanoids into what is known as modern man.

In other words, to be clear, Vlad did not take the apes and make them human. Another Creator God did that. Vlad did insert ET DNA into the evolving humans and make some of them part reptilian. Hence, the Rh negative bloodline.

But, as you now know, that is a repeated pattern throughout the universe. And as you know now, the corruption of scientists on a planet is a repeated pattern by Dracula as well. As you now understand many of the species throughout the universe are not all good, or all bad, like humans they have both among them; like humans, they have both inside of them.

VLAD DRACULA: GLADIOUS THE NEANDERTHAL

My only response to that piece of information is that the apes and Neanderthals were a highly inferior creation. The Seeker who is responsible for the earliest so-called evolution of the apes into humanoids is named Gladious. He is a simpleton. You've been told that Creator Gods create beings that reflect them. He is a Monkey Man and Merlin should have ousted him from the Seeker School, but because Merlin prefers to keep students around him that are inferior to him (so he can look good), he kept Gladious around. Gladious is not even worth my consideration. Inferior minds create inferior species. End of that story. End of the Neanderthals.

MERLIN: THE END OF DAYS AND REVELATIONS

This is the time for revelations. That is what these End Days signal—revealing the hidden stories behind the lies you have been told for so long. You are beginning to understand that you have been trapped on this planet for awhile. Some of you are feeling that perhaps you have all had your memories erased and replaced with false ones. There are many people who suffer from false memory syndrome, meaning that what you believe are your memories often times are not. Sorting out the truth from fiction is an enormous task. Many of you feel that your memory is being erased day to day. For some your experiences are virtual and held in the memory but are not physical/terrestrial.

Many of you are also beginning to awaken to the realization that your memories of childhood contain large blank pieces, or you are beginning to realize that you were abducted and "messed with" in your childhood, but the details are fuzzy. After WWII, when the Nazis were forced underground, large groups of human beings were put together for the sole purpose of using them as human guinea pigs. Stories abound of laboratories that are used for these genetic manipulations and DNA experimentation. The most famous revolve around Dulce, New Mexico and Montauk, New York. Some of these abductions are physical and some are virtual, meaning that sometimes the memory of actual human modern-day abductions are replaced with a memory of an alien abduction experience to confuse the abductee.. Sometimes the abductee is implanted with a false memory, which causes them to blame an innocent person for their experience.

The Starseeds are here to help awaken you to the truth at this End of Days. They are here to assist you to end the lies. Many of you might choose to remain imprisoned here, because you want to choose the Devil You Know. But, others of you will want to wake up and reclaim your right of sovereignty and step back into your true divine self. Many of you want to become, once again, human/divine beings.

You have witnessed in previous times how the Earth has been cleared of species and re-seeded with new species. You have heard tales of The Great Flood and seen how the dinosaurs were removed from Earth. Because of this you are aware that it is certainly possible for this to happen once again; and you await it. Some of you are eager for "doom and disaster," because you believe it will finally set you free. Others of you believe that the Galactic Federation, "would never let that happen," even in the face of overwhelming evidence that the Galactic Federation has allowed a great deal of doom and disaster to happen on this planet! Many of you believe that you will be rescued, because you are one of the "good" ones—and you define that as a "good Christian" or a "good Starseed," or a "good fill-in-the-blank."

The ones who control this prison planet, Vlad's army, know what you are thinking. They have invaded your both your dreams and your waking states. They control the media and the food supplies. They want you to be their robot army of hybrid aliens because that's what Vlad wants. And Vlad wants it because he wants me (Merlin) to realize that the human template—in fact every other Creator God's template—is inferior to his.

VLAD DRACULA: THE END OF DAYS

What are these End of Days? What are these days that bring with them the destruction and the punishing of the wicked and the ascension of the good? It has been told to you that only a mere handful will "make the cut." Why is that? Because most of you don't have a clue how to behave like the Ten Commandments have asked of you. Why? Because it is not your true nature. If it was your true nature, nobody would have to announce how to behave on a stone tablet, and threaten you with eternal damnation if you don't behave that way.

Are most of you behaving like your true nature? Are most of you enjoying your sinful ways? A resounding 'yes' is what I hear. How many of you are committing or have committed adultery? How many of you have lied, cheated or stolen? How many of you have judged your neighbor? How many of you support institutions that are corrupt? How many of you lust after power? How many of you don't honor your mother, your father or anyone else for that matter? How many of you own weapons designed for only one thing—murder?

That is your true nature. Perhaps there are only 144,000 among you that have never done those bad things and will be "saved." The rest of you, as far as I can tell, belong to me.

MERLIN: COPING WITH THE WAKE-UP CALL

The wake-up call is designed to lift all of you from your small-minded belief systems and to assist you to expand your consciousness in new ways. Every evolving species must move forward or die. How the species moves forward is determined both by its collective consciousness, and the determination of its Creator God. The Creator God listens to the species and helps them along the path of evolution. If a species wishes to move from third-dimensional density then the Creator God arranges the transition.

Creator God Vlad Dracula has obviously altered many of the creations throughout this universe.

On the Earth today are many humans who are playing Creator God without having any understanding of the ramifications of such experimentation. The ones such as the Nazi scientists understand to a greater extent what they are doing. They know they are playing God, and that is their intention. They are on what humans call an ego trip. It is the innocent DNA splicers and cloners, who think that it is their job to save a species, or alter a species, or save a life, that are the ones who work blindly. They are unaware of the arena they have just entered. They are unaware that they too are on an ego trip. Merely by dong this work they have inserted themselves into the Creator God arena, and if this book has shown you anything, it has made you aware that that is an arena that only the bravest and most fearless want to enter.

The Creator God wars are the Orion Wars, or as some have dubbed them, *Merlin's War*. Most human scientists have no idea what they are walking into. Rather than study life creation in a spiritually-based school such as mine, they think that life creation can be successfully learned separate from God. These scientists are prime targets for Vlad's energy and influence. Whether working in the underground laboratories, or working "out in the open," these people are headed for an experience not so different than was depicted in the famous movie, *Jurassic Park*. It was a story of creation run amok, fueled by ego and greed. These people say to themselves, "I think it needs to be done, so let's do it."

This brings me directly into my next issue: Thine will be done. What does that mean to any of you? Can you even conceive of such a notion? Let the Higher Self take over. Let the Higher Self decide? Most of you confuse this with inertia. Or you confuse it with losing control. But, you have no idea how to be both human and divine, meaning that you let your Higher Self pilot the ship. Craving leads you into action and into trouble. Your ego wants something, and convinces you that it is your right to have that thing or person.

Let me just remind you that you have absolutely no idea how to keep your own body alive. Your body's millions of chemical reactions which occur with each breath are done by your God Self. Not by your human mind. Now multiply that by an infinite number and that's the number of chemical reactions necessary at every millisecond to keep all of life sustained. None of you could keep one body successfully alive with your surface or ego mind. None of you. Yet you keep trying. You keep trying to do it better than God. You keep failing. And you will fail until you realize that there is a Force that has the innate intelligence to pilot all this for you, and if you listen to it first, and respect it, it will probably actually assist you to do the right thing.

Here is the wrong thing: Create a world so out of balance that species die out by the bucketful and then head for the laboratories to "save" these species or make new ones.

Here is the right thing: Listen to what nature needs to maintain balance and respect that. If you are all willing to do this, Vlad Dracula will immediately become powerless on this planet.

Is that so very hard? Yes, it seems. It's like someone who puts salt in their coffee by mistake, and keeps trying to fix it with more and more complex chemicals poured into the coffee to neutralize the salt, and sweeten it. Dump out the coffee and start over. Maybe that's what the Wake-up Call at the End of Days is all about. Maybe. Just consider that. You have the ability to step back, end the madness, listen to the needs of nature, and start again peacefully. If you do not, eventually the coffee will have to be dumped and re-poured. It's certainly been done before.

THE GREAT ANGELIC BEINGS OF LIGHT AND YOU

Many of you call on the Great Angelic Beings of Light to assist you with your spiritual work. Gabriel, Michael, Ariel, Raphael, Metatron, Sandalphon, Uriel are just a few of the angelic energies that assist the human race to remember their true origins. It is also true that some of you contain a divine ensouled spark of one of these angels. In other words, you have chosen to take a piece of a great archangel and bring it to the Earth within you. This allows you to carry their resonance into the dense reality of 3D the Earth and lift the vibration. The trick, of course, is not letting the Earth bring you down!

The angels you work with are involved in the Realms of Illuminated Truth, and they hold the remembrance of the Oneness of All Reality so that it can always be accessed and remembered. Without them holding heaven open it would be impossible for all of you to reconnect with your true home; Vlad's creational hell realm in the lower astral plane would be all that you knew. When you are connected to these beings you will be flooded with peace and a remembrance of your own divinity. They will never try to fool you into worshipping them or turning your power over to them. If they are real they empower you to become stronger. If they are real, they set you free to become a master of your own destiny.

Safety will never be achieved by running away from fear. Fear will follow you everywhere you go as long as it is held within you. Turn toward your fear, be like the great angels, and remember the truth of who you really are at the highest level. Because when I created the human race to be an ensouled race with the spark of angelic divinity within you, I made sure that you could always find your way home to heaven.

The secret to overcoming Vlad is not in fighting him with a sword made of metal. He is correct in saying that he controls the weapons on Earth. He made sure that his army of fierce, nasty and controlling beings created and retained control of the weapons, but he has an Achilles heel that most of you don't know about. This Achilles heel is what the archangels can show you: Love. Not human love, because that isn't strong enough to defeat Vlad. The key to making him shrink up and run from you in fear is Divine Love. Can you hold Unconditional Love? Can you hold Love in the face of fear for all things including Vlad? If you can face him and send him Love he will run from you, but if you send him hatred and fear he will draw closer.

Remember that you are angels incarnated. Remember your true nature, which is divine and loving. Remember, "They know not what they do." When you see Vlad and his army approaching you, send them all Love. The Light blinds his army. They run and scatter from it like cockroaches.

A summoning was done when Vlad Dracula was incarnated as Prince Vlad Dracula, or Vlad the Impaler. One day, after so many thousands of humans had been tortured by impalement, a summoning for the angels in heaven to approach was made. When the angels brought down the Light it blinded Vlad and his henchmen, and they fled the castle like rats off a burning ship. They couldn't tolerate the Light.

You cannot carry the Light if you do not love yourself. You must love your enemy as yourself. Even Jesus told you this. It means if you do not love yourself, you cannot hold enough love to defeat your enemy. If you cannot love yourself, you cannot love your enemy as yourself. If you love yourself you are able to find love for all things in the end. Vlad knows this and one of the reasons that you are constantly subjected to reasons not to love yourself (too tall, too short, too ugly, too fat, too dumb, and too poor) is that Vlad knows it will keep you away from the kind of love you need to defeat him. Your own self-loathing is his assurance that you will never find enough unconditional love to make him run the other way. It all begins with you loving yourself, and that begins with you doing and acting in a way that makes you love yourself.

If you are not in love with yourself, start there. It's all about what's inside; your outside is immaterial. When you die you will not evaluate your life based on the outside. A bigger or better car will not impress your spiritual self. What will impress your spiritual self is how much you loved others and yourself. What will really impresses your spiritual (angelic) self is how much you did that, even when others weren't nice to you. That's what will impress both you and your spiritual guides.

VLAD DRACULA:
UNDERSTANDING THE DARK MIND

There are many of you who struggle to understand the motivations of the dark mind. You can't imagine what is gained by working with the Dark Side. When told that there is a dark agenda (even after the Nazi agenda was exposed to you in World War II) you ask, "But who is doing this?" with an incredulous look on your face, as if your brain can't possibly wrap itself around the concept that someone actually wants to harm others to gain control or power.

It is strangely endearing, I will admit, to see how many of you staunchly refuse to look at the Dark Side as an organized group of individuals. You see it reflected in the institutions all around you. Your history is nothing but war and lust for power for as long as you can remember; but still like the Pollyanna's you are, you keep hoping that it will all just go away if you pretend it doesn't exist.

Let me tell you a little bit more about the structure of the Family of Dark. Like any organization it has levels, and much like your armies it contains a Supreme Commander, four star generals and on down. The foot soldiers are the ones who keep the energy alive throughout your communities by doing their witchcraft and voodoo, and by spreading fear with murder, rape, and torture. They work in town governments and politics to keep dissention and anger a driving force of separation. They wield darkness and fear at the local level. These foot soldiers in the war are expendable, as there always will be many more right behind them, willing to pick up the call.

That is much like your own military institutions. No matter how many times a young man is told by an older man that being a soldier means that you will be used, abused, and spit out by the army, there are an endless stream of young men indoctrinated into the idea that it makes you a more valuable person to go to war. Well, in my army it's quite similar. I don't even worry about revealing this to all of you, because it won't make a bit of difference. I'll still have plenty of recruits. Just like the army has plenty of recruits even when an endless stream of men return with one leg or arm or blinded or brain damaged. It doesn't stop the recruits from coming. So, this revelation will not stop the Family of Dark foot soldiers from signing up.

They, like your soldiers, suffer from the false belief that they are important, powerful, able to be the exception to the rule, and especially the false belief that they are tougher than they are. They may be bullies, my foot soldiers, but they are not truly powerful. They may think that their voodoo and black magic makes them my equal, but they are wrong. However, they want the opportunity to grow more powerful, to be my generals, so they keep trying to serve me, to please me and get me to promote them. A few do get promoted, of course, but the vast majority end up isolated, alone and struck down by their own badly-cast spells or ill-conceived power grabs.

It doesn't really matter to me. If they have stirred up fear and anger they are doing their job. However, I must add that neither I nor my generals tolerate failure, and if a member of the Family of Dark is given an assignment, and they do not succeed at that assignment, they will be punished in some manner. The smallest punishment is that support is withdrawn and they are on their own. The largest punishment is public humiliation and possible death. This is usually reserved for the big players on the world stage. If they are not performing as I hoped you will hear of their arrest, and they will either be forced from power or they will step down. All of this is done without sentimentality. I also have many ways of mentally torturing an individual, and bringing them to madness.

Anyone and everyone is expendable in my quest to establish myself as Supreme Ruler of the Universe. If my life as Vlad the Impaler did anything, it should have shown you that I am far from sentimental about these things! I do not allow loyalty to cloud my decisions. In that way I will succeed. I understand persuasion is more effective than force; but I will do what it takes.

I communicate with my generals and foot soldiers in a myriad of ways. I am able to insert into their thoughts the ideas that I want carried out. They know what to do. The biggest problem I have is that they often forget who it is they serve, and their arrogance becomes overwhelming. When I see this happening I will give them a swift reminder. When you "sell your soul to the devil" he always owns it, and if you forget that you are working for my benefit you will be reminded.

But, once again there are always plenty of people willing to "sell their souls." This is an actual contract that is presented, to a human being by another human being who works for me. The contract is presented, and if the human does not accept the contract immediately, they will be given a period of time to consider it. If the human does not take up the contract they will often die shortly afterwards. That is why these contracts are often presented in the hospital to individuals who are near death, promising them life is a strong motivator, and if they do not choose the contract it is easy to do away with them. Merlin told you that people who want fame or power or drugs are also candidates, and of course that is true. So, who is chosen for the contract presentation? Someone who is weak enough of character that we are about 99% sure they will accept the contract. Someone we know who wants something very badly. Someone we believe can be easily manipulated to join the Dark Side.

If you wish to join my army: The Winning Team, just holler. I'll hear you, and you will be visited. We are always on the outlook for recruits.

MERLIN: THE RETURN OF CYGNUS – THE WHITE DRAGON

Vlad continues to insist he is the winner of this Game. Doth he protest too much? The reason he wants this book to be realized is because he cannot stand to be an unrecognized winner. It's no fun to win but no one knows it. However, this game of chess has more moves in it, and I can see a different outcome.

The constellation of Cygnus contains the energy of the White Dragon, or the angelic energy of the Higher Realms as expressed through the energy of the White Dragon. It is not the swan that delivers to you the energy blasts that will awaken your DNA, and bring you back to your fully awakened human state. It is the energy of the White Dragon.

It is easy to imagine that a constellation of a swan and a dragon could resemble each other, both have broad wings stretched out far from the body, and both have a long neck. But the energy of the White Dragon is far more powerful than the energy of a swan, and that is needed to awaken the human template once again. The truth of Cygnus was hidden from humanity.

The Greek God Orpheus was a direct descendent of the White Dragons, and so it is that he is said to have returned to the constellation Cygnus when he died with his lyre (the constellation of Lyra) beside him. The powerful energy of the White Dragon is available to those who connect to Cygnus. Cygnus, also known as the Northern Cross, is the intersecting of the dimensions. Through the portal of Cygnus (the White Dragon) one can move into heaven and beyond. What is this intersection? It is the wedding of the dark and the light, the down and the up, the yin and the yang, male and female. At the intersection of the Northern Cross lies the end to duality and polarity—the blending of oppositional forces.

It appears that this battle of wits is simply between Vlad and me, and that you have little to do with it. Perhaps you feel that you are merely chess pieces on the game board, and that the major players determine where it is you will move. But, this is not accurate. Indeed, there are Creator Gods who have access to timelines, information, and wisdom that has eluded you. However, your free will always determines the next move. You stand at the brink of everything. Each of you is making a choice that not only impacts your individual lives but the lives of everyone around you everywhere. And you ask: What is that choice?

The choice is: What master will you serve?

Ah Ha!! For a moment you thought I meant either Merlin or Vlad didn't you? Fess up. That's how you are programmed. I did not. What I meant is that you making a choice to take full responsibility for your actions and the life you create, or you are choosing to remain a victim to the forces of fear, hatred and denial.

Choose wisely my friends—your future depends upon it.

PART II
The Human Journey: My Journey

This is Margaret talking to you now, and I wish to share with you, human to human, some of the understandings and insights I have come across in my journey to awaken from the old paradigms. Each one of us has our own journey to be sure, but the more we share, the more we find out that our journeys are not as dissimilar as we might think. I believe one of the things the Family of Dark fears the most is the sharing of our personal insights and experiences without fear. That is why in countries where fascism is quite evident, censorship is too.

If we wish to break out of the Matrix of control we must begin to talk to one another freely. We must begin to share our stories without fear. Our stories empower others to share their stories, and empowerment is what the escape is all about.

Most of you who are reading this book have learned many new things from other books, the internet and friends, and at times have felt yourselves to be overwhelmed by the information that is coming into the world at amazing rates. It can be difficult to discern truth from fiction, and of course as Merlin makes quite clear, this is what Vlad wants.

In this section I wish to speak a bit about my own journey, and also to tie some of the *Part One* information into the writings and teachings that many of you are aware of, including those of David Icke, Jordan Maxwell, Barbara Marciniak, Patricia Cori and others; writings that have been challenging us, and at times confusing us, but always stimulating us to new ideas. (If you are unfamiliar with these writers you might enjoy checking them out to further stimulate some new thoughts and ideas.) That is what makes us grow. At least for the time being, in the United States we are allowed to write things, and self-publish them, so that others can have access to information. However, in many places this is not possible. Let's take advantage of our freedom and stretch our minds. Just as Merlin says, "this information is **not** given to you as Truth, but to stimulate the Truth that lies within you."

I began my journey to awakening in 1984 when I met a man who stimulated in me a vision of a past life we had together. In the vision I was standing next to a fireplace wearing a green dress that reached to the floor, and it was clearly a different century. The room I was standing in appeared to be the drawing room, or receiving room for guests, and the guest I was receiving made my heart pound. It was him, the man I was meeting for the first time in 1984. Neither of us looked like we do today, but I just "knew" it was us; the energy, the feelings, it was all there.

What does this have to do with today? What does this have to do with my life? Why am I having these visions? The person who saved me by helping me to understand what was happening was Shirley MacLaine. She had the strength to share the stories of her personal life even though the Lower Matrix controlled media laughed at her. I am always deeply indebted to her for her courage to speak out at a time when much of this was very new (at least to Western minds), and the vast majority of humanity was still snoozing. She truly went, *Out on a Limb* as her book was titled.

But why was I having these visions? I was having these visions to awaken me to another state of consciousness. I had started the journey of remembering who I was. I had begun to step out of the Lower Matrix that said, "You are limited to one body, one time on Earth," and see myself as Spirit capable of manifesting different form. That was my first step down the Rabbit Hole, and at the time it was so enormous, it almost overwhelmed me completely. But, my

Higher Self was smart. I made sure along the way I surrounded myself with at least a few people who were willing to listen and understand, people who "got it." This is not a journey you want to take alone. So, if you are going down the Rabbit Hole, make sure you take a few traveling companions.

It is becoming more and more evident to everyone that something big is happening on planet Earth. It's hard to deny unless you are a master at denial (which of course many people are.) As we search for explanations we are confronted with tremendous amounts of contradictory information, all of which contradicts what we were raised to believe as a whole in our society. Now, I understand I'm talking about being raised in America in the twentieth century as a "baby boomer." If I was raised in Nigeria, or Russia, or East Germany, I would be telling quite a different story and speaking from a different point of view. When I was a child in 1966, I lived in Hamburg, Germany, and at the age of eleven I got to see the border between East and West Germany. Huge towers with armed guards prevented people from entering and leaving. Land mines peppered the ground, and barbed wire made sure to stop you if the other things failed. If I had been raised behind those land mines I would be telling you a different story, because the illusion of freedom would not have entered my consciousness. I would have had real prison bars to stare at, not merely emotional and mental ones, and I would have known I was not free.

American children were not told about any of this going on in other parts of the world, and if we were, it was told to us in a fairy tale kind of way—the big bad wolf was out there somewhere in the world, but don't worry children, the big bad wolf isn't in America. We were coddled and cared for, and when we knew about children who weren't being taken care of we ignored them, because it was too upsetting to the view of Mother, God and Apple Pie that was being crammed down our collective throats. Certainly I didn't know anything about what was going on with the Nuclear Energy Commission and the fact that the United States was doing nuclear testing that was so dangerous that even Robert Oppenheimer and Werner Von Braun (Hitler's scientist/consultant) refused at times to participate. Oppenheimer was fired for being disloyal because of his moral refusal to participate in nuclear testing that might have destroyed all life. (Anyone interested in the history of this can read the book *Area 51* for information which has been released now as unclassified.) As elementary school children all we knew was to hide under our desks for protection.

The truth that we live in a country that was playing with nuclear weapons, and testing them like a ten-year-old boy plays with firecrackers, should make all of us realize that our world leaders are children in "big boy" bodies and we must admit to ourselves that we have given them power over us. Why? Because we wanted to believe in the fantasy that they care about us; it makes us feel safe.

I come from a family of non-believers in religion; some call them atheists (statistically the most hated group in America by the way.) So, although I myself have always been deeply spiritual (I dressed as an angel when I was a child) I was alone in those spiritual beliefs. The belief in angels came with me when I arrived on Earth. For a short while my father took us to the Unitarian church to try to give us something, but we were taught about evolution and the planets not about Jesus. About Jesus I was told, "He was a good man and you should try to do unto others as they would do onto you." In my family morality was separate from religion. Be a good person because that's the way you are supposed to be; not because some devil is going to poke you with a pitchfork.

I never stepped foot in a church, unless it was a cathedral in Europe to stare at the amazing architecture in wonder. To me church was a tribute to the medieval beliefs of humanity. Religion was historical; something that controlled the world in the olden days but not in modern times. In modern America we were free to believe what we wanted to, because weren't we in the Land of the Free?

Now, if I had been raised as a Mormon, or Jehovah's Witness, or Catholic, or even as a Jew I would be telling a vastly different story. Try to break away from those groups and you will often lose your support system called your family. Your parents will either tell you that you are going to hell and they can't be associated with you anymore, or they will moan and groan at your decision. Why? Why?

So, this freedom of religion was certainly foreign for many people. It might be a nice idea they would tell you, but try it from the inside of a Mormon temple and then we'll talk. Religion has been one of the most effective prisons for both mind and body ever conceived. It has locked you in fear so that you don't explore other ideas, and if the fear of hell wasn't enough to convince you, it used shunning, and the threat of being disowned from needed support systems of family and community, to complete the task. Did we really need armed guards and barbed wire and land mines? We had church and school to lock our minds away. And that was before we were drugged and frequency controlled with cell phones and cell towers. That was before the alien abductions and the MK Ultra mind control programs; that was when we believed that the Nazi doctors, leaders, and scientists had been defeated, and didn't know that they merely got paid to come to the United States, and Russia to continue their work. That was when we believed in a government who told us these Nazi men were our enemies, not on our payroll.

A friend of mine, a social worker, once told me of a psychological experiment that was performed on kittens. They were born and raised behind bars. Because of this they didn't perceive the bars until they had bumped into them. I concluded that if you are raised on a prison planet you are not going to know it; until someone or something makes you aware of it. Your existence will seem completely natural to you, until you "wake up" to the bars that are right in front of your nose.

But, as American children we were the innocents in the Land of the Free. The Nazis had been defeated, and the suburbs were being built. We were told to learn our lessons, go to church and school and memorize what we were being tested on, and don't ask too many questions. Then the 60's happened.

My older sister and I would laugh and say that everyone lost their virginity at the same time, no matter how old they were, in 1968 or 1969. Hell No We Won't Go! Pictures of the Vietnam War reached my teenage eyes; images of toxic chemicals being thrown on innocent children to burn them and torture them. We were forced to grow up pretty quickly. I cried a lot in those days as I watched those television pictures, and I wondered if I could live in a world with so much hatred and pain. Martin Luther King, Jr. took a stand to free "his people," and the students at Kent State were gunned down during peaceful protests. America was changing. America was waking up.

Well, we can't have that, can we? Have you noticed that

every time people begin to "wake up" the control systems use the same methods to clamp down? Right before WWI there was a renaissance. One of the most exciting and creative periods of human history was the end of the nineteenth century. Brilliant minds were at work in all fields of endeavor. Did you learn that in school? Artists, musicians, philosophers, scientists were discovering how to see the world through new eyes. Women demanded the right to vote. Can't have all those new ideas floating around like that, can we? WWI made a good attempt to end human liberation but then came the nineteen twenties; girls lifted their skirts and began to smoke and vote. In the twenties artists, painters, and writers were prolific, and the Surrealists and Dadaists pushed the envelope of human thought. Can't have that can we? The great depression followed by the rise of Hitler and WWII focused everyone once again on issues of survival. After the war Joseph McCarthy made sure than anyone who dared to think outside the box in America was put into fear or punished.

From the fifties onward the Nazi scientists went to work in earnest, and it wasn't just on weapons of mass destruction (as we like to call them today.) In the 70's while most of us were turning the heart-centered 60's into the 70's of group sex, drugs and mindless disco dancing, the Montauk project, Los Alamos, and Dulce, NM were in full swing. These underground laboratories were staffed by the neo-Nazi scientists, from our taxes, to invent new and ingenious ways to keep us asleep or kill us. Having read on the internet numerous reports about Dulce, NM, and its underground bases I decided to pay this remote Apache reservation a visit. After visiting Dulce, NM myself I have no doubt that most of what is said about it on the internet is true. A friend of mine who works in New Mexico with the Native American population as a drug and alcohol counselor was shocked when I told him I'd gone there. "No one goes to Dulce," he said. It is a wasteland; in Dulce it felt that not only the people, but the Earth herself had died.

Are you seeing a pattern here? Somebody doesn't want you to be awake. Somebody wants you to be too afraid to change the way you think and perceive of yourself. Someone is desperate enough to keep that from happening, and they will do almost anything to prevent it. That someone is not just an allegorical figure. The vampires are real.

"How can that be?" you ask. "There can't be a group that organized. That's conspiracy theory. That's paranoid." Go live in East Germany in the 60s, and then talk conspiracy theory. Go back to Germany in the 30's, and then we will talk conspiracy theory. Go live in Russia in the 70's, and then we will talk conspiracy theory. Go live in China or Afghanistan and try to speak out against the government, or go live in America and stop believing what you've been spoon-fed, and then we will talk conspiracy theory. All over the world there is evidence of repression and restriction. The illusion of freedom is a privilege few are allowed to experience.

Someone wants you enslaved, and it obviously means a lot to them to keep that going. Around the world (America included) if the rulers wanted you to have enough money, food, and jobs to survive well then you would. There is plenty for everyone as long as one percent of the population doesn't hold 99% of the wealth and power. Today that is the statistic that expresses our reality: Occupy Wall Street woke us up to the understanding that the 99% are being manipulated by only 1% of the world's population.

Okay, so *Part One* of the book told you a fairy tale you think. There isn't a real Dracula. He is a cartoon. Some of you might remember a scene from the movie the *Matrix* when the Oracle tells the hero Neo what's going to happen to him. Then she offers him a fresh-baked chocolate chip cookie and says, "Don't worry, Neo, when you step out that door you'll remind yourself you don't believe any of this stuff and you'll start to feel better."

Many of us are beginning to hold on to what the Oracle told us, and are refusing to be put asleep by the chocolate chip cookies.

It is not my intention to expound on every detail of every so-called conspiracy theory out there, and if you are interested in any of these things, the internet is full of theories and ideas. Some are true and some are not true; that's up to you to decide. But people such as David Icke and Jordan Maxell have devoted their lives to pushing the envelope. Jesse Ventura has even done a TV show called *Conspiracy Theory* exposing these things. Whether you agree with these people or not they are a force for change in the modern world. For those of you coming upon all of this for the first time now, you are actually coming onto the deck of a ship that has been at sea for awhile, even though you've never even known the ship existed. For example,

David Icke and Jordan Maxwell have both been talking about the reptilian and ET agendas for decades.

But, I am here to explain to you who and what is behind the seeming "human" agenda, and what is even behind the reptilian agenda. I am here to help you understand that those beings are slaves to something even bigger than they are. The Master of Fear is Dracula. He is not a cartoon character. The vampires that are beginning to crop up everywhere around you are doing his bidding. They just introduced *Vampire* perfume. Young children are encouraged to play with a new line of vampire dolls. Teenagers are seduced by the *Twilight* series. Need I say more?

If they are vampires, then they must need us to survive. That is the nature of a vampire. They need us. So, who's in the driver's seat now? Is it really them or is it us? The first clue to our empowerment is the realization that without us they die. If they can't get nourishment from the Divine Matrix and need to get it from other humans, then if we refuse to feed them they die. That is *Clue # 1 To Our Empowerment*: Stop feeding them. Confront them face-to-face, tell them you know what they are up to, and say you will not participate.

THE JOURNEY CONTINUES

I was afraid of Dracula instinctively since childhood. Until adolescence I slept with the covers up to my chin to keep my neck from being exposed. I think I brought that in with me too. Children know things that adults pretend they don't know. Children know that the fourth dimension, although unseen, is alive with much activity. Children know that fairies and goblins are real.

I'm furious when I hear parents talk about the fact that children's fears are just manipulations. "Oh, my daughter keeps saying that something bad is in her room, but I know it's just her manipulating me so I let her cry all alone in the dark." She's three years old for God's sake! Protect her, honor her, and love her! Realize that she is still awake to the subtle realms and has not yet become as cut-off to non-physical reality as you are.

When I look back at my early childhood I realize that even then I was being given all I would need to do my "task" in the world, and

I can assure you, so were you. Your karma, your fears, your loves, your hates—they were reflecting to you what it was you needed to "tackle and take on." There are no accidents.

Clue # 2 to our Empowerment: Something is bigger than even Dracula. Something he doesn't want you to see. Something that will always give you what you need to awaken, if you are brave enough to take the journey.

As a child I sent in a picture to a television playschool show called Romper Room. The wall of the school was covered with pictures that children had sent in to remind other children how to behave. Things like, "Never cross the street alone." "Never take candy from strangers." Those kinds of messages and pictures peppered the wall.

I wrote, "Never push an angel." The picture I drew was of an angel being pushed by a bully. When I was four or five years old I donned my angel costume and confronted the seven and eight-year-old boy bullies on my block, "Never push an angel," I informed them without fear. Even today I am saying the same thing. The Family of Dark has attacked me many, many times but I always remind them, "Never push an angel."

Clue #3 to our Empowerment: We are not who we think we are. We have all had many powerfully positive and negative experiences throughout our lives, and we have all been assisted by our spiritual guides to understand and grow from these experiences. Many people have also had very, very bad experiences and have been abused and overwhelmed by depression, sorrow, and drug or alcohol addiction. What is it that allows one person to "rise above" the experiences of their lives, and another to "fall below" them?

In simple terms it is ego. Extreme self-identification, or identification with the lower self, is a trap that ensnares all of us into misery. It should become evident to any thinking person that the world, in many ways, is moving into greater and greater materialism and superficiality. Our economic survival is dependent on people wanting and needing more things outside of themselves to feel happy and good. These technological gadgets are bringing more chaos and envy, and less satisfaction to the human spirit, while at the same time our natural environment is being eroded by corporations who spill oil and dump nuclear waste and by traffic and noise that make it increasingly difficult to find a place outdoors that is actually noise and pollution free.

If you couple this with the frequency control devices and the chemical spraying that is being done all over the world (chemtrails), even reaching into wilderness lands on every continent, you can see that finding a pristine place on the Earth can be quite a challenge.

So, here we sit awakening to our multi-dimensional selves, and yet lifting the veil on the underbelly world all around us. It appears that we are uncovering the upper dimensions, and the lower dimensions, all at the same time. When I first began uncovering past lives I also began to notice how the barriers between good and evil break down. I wrote the book, *Infinite Darkness/Infinite Light* to reveal this idea to others. In the book the heroine (based on myself) goes through a personal struggle to understand and heal the past lives she uncovers, and free herself from an obsessive love affair. As she uncovers the past lives, she discovers she was a Jewish woman, and that the man she is in love with today, was a Nazi in that past life. In that life he impregnated her, and they were both killed for it.

Another vision brings her the discovery that she was a sexually-abused young boy in a life in ancient Rome, who grew up to become an angry and abusive Roman man. The heroine of the book sees that each of us is good and bad, dark and light and that our moment of redemption is often our darkest moment. It is when we are in the darkness that we reach for the light.

When people do past life journeys they become whole for that very reason. It shakes them from the complacency and compartmentalization of, "I'm good, you're bad," and requires them to create a new and expanded self-identity. If you have been "bad" in another life it makes it much easier to forgive the "bad" in others and heal the wounds of separation between you. Many people realize that if they over-identify with being black, white, red or yellow, they believe in a lie—the lie of the ego. Scratch the surface and you will find that underneath every white person is the skin of all the races. We are all one.

Those in control of the Lower Matrix do not want you to find this out. If you do then you will not hate everyone else like they want you to. If you understand that you have been all things, and that all of humanity is linked together, then you might start to love one another and become focused on helping rather than hurting.

Those who cannot rise above the ego-identification of victim and perpetrator, and refuse to look at their enemy and love them as themselves, are destined to be locked into the battle of duality and hatred. The reptilians and vampires need you to argue and hate because they feed off the energetic residue of these emotions. Have you ever noticed that chaos creators are so good at it that they will enter a room and suddenly everyone and everything is topsy-turvy and upsetting? These beings need the chaos to survive upon, and the best way to create chaos is fear and separation.

If you believe that the big, bad guy is always the guy across the border, then this keeps the war alive. When you begin the journey to release yourself from the Lower Matrix it will always take you away from ego-identification, until you can embrace all aspects of the self and forgive them.

Know thyself. It's what Dracula definitely doesn't want you to do. Where is the vampire within you? All these "bad guys" are mirroring our own "bad guy." Before you go attacking the bad guys outside of you, clear up the bad guy within you. As a past life regression therapist for many years I am a great believer that the healing is in the shadow.

Clue #4 to our *Empowerment*: As above so below. God is within us. Everything that is, exists everywhere, and nowhere. The more we begin to understand how reality works, the more we can see that the model for it exists in the same form above and below, inside and outside, and up and down. If you study the human body, and the galaxies that make up the universe, you will see the same patterns and shapes in both. As above, so below. Everything is constructed from the same material.

Duality has required that we split this reality into two false realities. It required that we pretend that it isn't all one thing, expressing itself over and over in a myriad of identical ways, but that there are factions of difference within our reality. The false hologram of duality becomes clear when we are able to step out of our human identities, and access our Higher Selves.

The New Age took advantage of the fact that many of us had become unhappy with the old paradigms of religion. We were told a Harmonic Convergence had happened and this awakening was going to herald something new for mankind. As we considered ideas that we could talk to angels and channel them, or read tarot cards, or heal with crystals and stones, we began to believe that we knew the true path (at last), and that everything that spoke of angels, crystals, vortexes, healing, and spirit had to be the path to our enlightenment and liberation. Free, free at last! Thank God Almighty I'm free at last!

Wrong.

Because we did not understand the shadow, we had no idea what we were really liberating ourselves from. People embraced these new ideas but had not yet healed their fear, and they were awakening to only one side of the equation. This allowed many people who were working to keep us asleep to infiltrate the New Age movement and work from the "inside." These people would use catch words to hook us into their mind control programs and false religions: words such as miracles, spirit, oneness, love, empowerment, truth and ascended masters. Even the CIA got into the act and designed pseudo-religions that were supposed to liberate us, but did not. Why? Most likely to further the understandings of mind control.

Most people believe that the use of certain catch words indicate that they are in the presence of a good person. Many of us continue to look outside ourselves for God, because we have forgotten that we live in an illusionary world. We forgot that there is only one thing—God—creating and recreating itself over and over. What is the real meaning of, as above, so below? God must be inside of us. We must look inside to find the meaning of God.

The difference between a cult and a spiritually-based program is that a spiritually-based program will not force you to believe in something as truth; it will encourage you to go on your own path to discover your truth. A true spiritual teacher is never threatened because you think or perceive differently. Unlike a cult you will not be punished or ostracized for thinking on your own and being different.

Unfortunately, being so deeply asleep and stuck within the Lower Matrix, we could not tell what was good and what was bad. Or to put it more accurately we couldn't tell what was leading us to true liberation and what was leading us further into slavery. The reptilian agenda of control, led by Dracula, was certainly not going to throw their hands up and say, "Oh, okay, you win." The vast majority of us had no idea that there was an organized group working to keep us enslaved. Until writers such as David Icke, and Barbara Marciniak and Patricia Cori began to speak about the Annunaki and reptilian agenda, and collect stories of human/reptilian shapeshifters throughout the world, the concept was inconceivable to most of us. And it still is.

That's where my personal experience has assisted me. (Remember you are given what you need to complete your tasks.) I was given a reptilian friend who, in great anger, shape-shifted before my eyes. Needless to say at the time I did not know what I was seeing, and all I did was run away in fear. But, because I did see it, I believe that the stories of reptilian shape-shifting are true. David Icke speaks about this at great length in his books. Many of you have reptilian parents, boyfriends, and girlfriends, and you know what I'm talking about: The eyes that become slits and the bodies and faces that appear to morph into almost demonic-looking beings.

The battle that began in heaven between the dragons arrived on the Earth a long time ago. We are now those dragons because we are fighting the war; I have seen my enemy and he is me. We are waging a war that we have long forgotten; a war that arose from the first fall of the angels. The fact that the reptilians have been interbred with humans means that they are now both inside and outside of us, just as God is.

Clue #5 to our Empowerment: Things are not as they appear to be. Because the supposed solid, third dimension is the dimension we were told to trust, most of us were raised to doubt any experience we had that couldn't be touched. We were told "seeing is believing" and "you can't trust your feelings." That left many of us at war with our intuition, which is the language of the Higher Self. That meant if someone said the right things (and smiled while saying them), then they were nice people and we should trust them, even if our bodies told us differently.

Many times our bodies would be having one reaction—discomfort—while our minds were trying to talk us out of it. That is what allowed many children to be sexually abused by so-called trusted adults. If our bodies were feeling icky, our minds were telling us that he is a priest, or a teacher, or a minister, or an uncle, so we should trust him despite what our instincts are telling us. The inability to trust our hearts and our instincts, and the re-enforcement by society that our minds are the only things that know the truth, kept us feeling split between our own truth and truth we saw outside ourselves.

A type of schizophrenia resulted from this, and we went to war with ourselves. We doubted our own ability to know what it was we thought, and we needed constant reassurance to know if what we thought, or felt, had merit. As a result of this we became weak and disassociated. We gave our power away to other people to tell us how to live, and what our truth should be. Young children who are different are often bullied, not only by other students, but by teachers as well; toe the line or risk being laughed at. In an environment like that it is very hard to establish your own identity. Very few parents are themselves liberated enough to encourage true liberation in their children. They want their children to fit in, have friends, get along, do well in school, and be a part of a society that most children understand quite early on is riddled with contradictions and hypocrisy.

Sex is the biggest example. Sexual exploitation is rampant in our society, and yet adults still pretend that it isn't. Children are being sexualized at younger and younger ages and paraded around in pageants, and yet they are told that sex is bad. So, we are born into a deeply divided schizophrenic world; told what to say and think in order to get along, and all the while fighting to make sense of it. Children are committing suicide. What does that tell us?

There are many people who have felt "outside the box," since early childhood. There are many children who had experiences that they were afraid to speak about for fear that they would be ridiculed or punished. Whether these experiences came from the humans that were supposed to keep them safe or from strangers, it didn't seem to matter; children often don't speak about the abuses they suffer until they are adults.

Because I had a relatively happy childhood I wasn't aware of the enormity of these problems until I began to work as a healer. As a young child I had a number of experiences where sexually-ill college students would masturbate in a car and wave me over to them; in sixth grade a girlfriend and I were sexually attacked in a parking lot and escaped by running away. In college, men would date rape me, and my friends. But, these were experiences that I could cope with. I had a safe family environment, and slept soundly at night without the fear of being harmed (except maybe from Dracula on the fourth dimension.)

Becoming a healer opened up my world to how much abuse is really out there. I am sure that any therapist will tell you the same thing. The stories that have been repressed in childhood (and often in adulthood) so desperately want to emerge, and a trusted healer will be asked to help hold these experiences and share them. Through the many people I have seen in over twenty years I became aware of a different level of reality.

This reality includes memories of what appear to be alien abductions and implantation. The memories are far more prevalent than any of us realize. As people are awakening to these memories they are realizing that there is an organized team of people who kidnap children and perform experiments on them and brutalize them. It is easy to get your hands on orphans who are abandoned in poor countries, but what about the stories of the elite who gave their children willingly to these neo-Nazi-alien driven scientists? These stories are also beginning to emerge, and these people talk about their experiences with frightening similarity. If we can allow ourselves to admit that the human experiments didn't stop in 1945, we can imagine that instead of rounding people up into concentration camps to experiment on them, all that changed was that now the experiments were in secret, underground labs.

Sounds like Vlad's siege throughout the universe landed on the Earth doesn't it? Are all these people crazy? Is this a worldwide shared delusion? Or just possibly are these people telling the truth? Are people really being pulled from their beds and taken to spaceships or laboratories? Are we really being experimented on and robotized? Are we really under attack in ways that we have been too afraid to listen to? I always tell people that everything makes sense when you have collected all the information. If it doesn't make sense we just don't have all the information yet.

To free ourselves we must admit that things are not what they appear to be and honor the experiences of other people, even when they stretch our imagination to the limit. Don't dismiss other people because they have had a weird experience. You might find that considering it as truth actually liberates something inside of you. Things are definitely not what they appear to be to the Lower Matrix consciousness.

Clue #6 to our Empowerment: The bad guys can help us grow spiritually as much as the good guys. I was a dancer from the age of 4 to 31. I danced every day of my life taking ballet and then modern dance classes. I was devoted to the art and defined myself as a dancer first and a person second (as they tend to do). Everything was about dance and choreography and expressing through the human body. In the 1980's I was on the Theater Arts faculty at Brown University and taught dance, choreography and dance history classes until a car accident changed that.

In 1986 on November 22nd, at the age of 31, I was hit by a drunk driver. The most interesting thing about this was that I had a premonition in the form of a dream the night before. In the dream, a car hit the back end of my car, and my car flew off the highway into a ditch…I awoke before the end of the dream. Even back then I knew that there was something very important about that dream, and I intuitively felt that it was an Exit or Death Point, and I was making a decision to exit the Earth or take the next leg of my journey. I said to two people that day (including the person I saw right before the accident), "I feel like I'm going to die, but I don't think I'm going to die. I think I have something to learn and I'm strong enough to learn it."

Boy was I right about that! The first thing that I had to integrate was that the accident was a choice I made. That I knew it was coming, somehow had agreed to it, and chose the outcome. That was not a popular point of view in 1986. At that time there were victims or perpetrators, and you were clearly one or the other.

My car did careen off the Interstate, down a hill and into a ditch. It was early in the morning around 2:00 a.m., and I was coming back alone from hearing a band play at a club. I managed to crawl out the passenger's side and up the embankment. Fortunately I was wearing a white coat, and could be more easily seen on the side of the road. The first car I waved down at that hour was a wonderful nurse who tended to me. The second car was an off-duty policeman who could radio for help. (Remember this was 1986 and nobody had cell phones.) I was rescued by human angels.

What stuck with me for a few days after the accident, while I lay around in my neck brace, was the immense feeling of evil and darkness that had washed over me when the drunk driver struck my vehicle at over 100 miles per hour. I realize now that the driver was carrying Vlad's energy; but at the time all I knew was that I had been introduced to a darkness I didn't know existed prior to that crash. It was a darkness that was almost overwhelming.

The car accident thrust me from my career as a dancer and into a career as a massage therapist. At first I moved to New York City thinking I could pursue a career as a choreographer, and did some commercial choreography but it became evident to me when I no longer could do the same level of dancing myself (my arabesque was shot) that it was time to move on. I chose massage therapy (I thought) because it helped me so much to recover from my injuries.

Enter my husband, Chris. Two years prior he had been on his way to massage therapy school in New York City. As he was entering the revolving door his angel tapped him on the shoulder and said clearly in his ear, "It's not the right time." He continued to revolve around the door and found himself back on the street saying, "It's not the right time."

Two years later on the New York City subway he looked over at me, a complete stranger on the same subway car, and said, "I'll bet she is going to massage therapy school, and she and I are going to be good friends." He got off two stops before I did to pick up school supplies, and when he entered the classroom there I was. We were not only good friends, we were soul mates. The angels brought us together to do this work to heal ourselves and others.

The "good guys" are there for you and sometimes the "good guys" are the "bad guys." If I hadn't been hit by the drunk driver I would have found it hard to leave the world of dance to start all over again. I'm so grateful that I did! That evil pushed me to the greatest good of my life. Many of you have found the same force at work in your own life. What are the blessings, the lessons, and the gifts of the experience? The darkness will push you to the light if you let it; which leads us to Clue Number Seven.

Clue #7 to our Empowerment: It really pisses Vlad off when he tries to hurt you and it backfires. I have been attacked by angry, bitter people (all of us have), and then I have been attacked by Vlad Dracula's helpers. The difference between the two types of attacks is that the first ones are done by wounded people who use their wounding as an excuse to wound others. They are not conscious of wounding you, and they would feel bad if they knew how much they had hurt you. Of course these people are *all* of us, and no one is immune from saying things they regret later. Perhaps some people do it more easily and more often than others. But we are all wounded, and we all strike out at times and have regrets later.

    Sometimes people also carry dark energy, and entity attachments, in their auric field. These attachments are the energetic residue of unfinished business, and angry people that exist in the etheric, fourth dimensional lower astral plane. Those of you who have hurtful family members or friends will recognize when a dark cloud seems to come over them and they act from their lower self. It is their wounding that allows this similar type of dark energy to be drawn to them, and to be expressed through them. This is what is known as an entity attachment or a dark energy attachment. Sometimes when you argue with someone it is the entities that argue through each of you, and when an argument escalates uncontrollably you can be pretty sure that is what is happening. You will always see this when you are dealing with an addict; that is why reasoning with one is almost impossible. But, if you are aware of this condition you have a greater chance of defusing it.

    The second type of attack is intentioned and thought out. These are the witches and wizards who enjoy doing Vlad's bidding. They study the use of black magic through many lifetimes, and they do rituals to strengthen their power. Now, if we lived in some third world countries this would be evident. Witches go door-to-door, like in the fairy tales, and bring you "poisoned apples." No one who has experienced this first hand would doubt the existence of these witches. But, in good ole' USA most of us believe that is paranoid "bulldoody," and just to speak of it brings scorn. Maybe, just maybe, there are a few people who practice black magic or Satanism, someone might agree, but it has nothing to do with the real world.

    These witches and wizards are conscious members of the Family of Dark, and sometimes they have status, rank, and membership in a secret society that knows far more than the innocents would ever imagine. I myself never believed in the Family of Dark as a conscious and organized group before my many (unwanted) human experiences with them. I can actually defend the point of view that for a long time, (at least before I lost my innocence) the Family of Dark has known me better than I know myself. That is because on this Earth, in this dimension, as Vlad has so clearly told you, they hold the cards. They are not afraid of the truth, because they have held the power to put you in fear. It is my destiny to write this book and reveal the truth about Vlad Dracula; I do it not to scare you, but to give you another point of view. You decide what you want to believe, but I have had too many experiences over the years to doubt that there is something beyond the reality we see daily.

The Family of Dark gives us gifts and strengthens us—they challenge us, frighten us, and make us rise to become the strongest, bravest people we can be—if we meet the challenge. At every moment they give us the opportunity to flee like scared rabbits or face them like powerful warriors. It's our choice; do we flee or meet the challenge. Are we mice, or are we Warriors of Light?

I don't know what will happen in the future. But, I'm sure that everything is a gift. Even the bad things can have blessings attached, and that really pisses Vlad off. That is why he had to demonize Lucifer who teaches us to find the light in the darkness.

I do know that I owe it to all of you to share a bit of my reality and my truth with you, without fear. Why? Why should I share this seeming "out there" point of view with people so openly? I do this in the hope that it will benefit all of you, and you will feel brave enough to share your truth and "out there point of view" with others. Together we wake up the world from this false Matrix. It has always been my belief that the brave ones show the truth of themselves without fear. By doing this they liberate others; this is what we all must emulate.

So, the Family of Dark strengthens us, and brings out fearlessness in us we didn't know we had. When you are attacked use it as a springboard to reach for the Light, and raise your vibration so they can't "get you." Be a Buddha of your own making.

Inside each and every one of us is a warrior of great courage and strength. If we release our fear they have nothing to "grab onto." To release your fear—face it. To free yourself from fear—face it. Your own fear will be used against you to disempower you. Free yourself from fear, and they have no way to bring you down. Those people you most admire throughout history did not let fear stop them from their tasks. I have not let fear stop me from this task. I ask that you join me in taking a courageous stance to uphold that which sets us all free. Do not let the light be a prison anymore than you allow the dark to be your prison. If you fear the dark you become imprisoned by the light because you are afraid of looking at the full spectrum of truth. It is time that we step from these prison walls.

And that, by the way, includes the Family of Dark. Because whether they know it or not, they too are enslaved by Dracula.

Clue #8 to our Empowerment: Vlad is the shadow side of human nature. Vlad Dracula is our collective shadow. He is the representative of all of our lower natures, and our vampire selves. There is no one on the Earth who is immune. The first thing you must do is stop hero-worshipping. If you don't need people to be perfect to love them you will (at last) begin to love yourself.

When you need your heroes to be better than you are, you weaken both yourself and your hero. Equality is essential to freedom. That means that you honor their gifts, and you honor your own. If we are to free ourselves from our shadow we have to stop elevating one another and then beating each other up for "letting us down."

The Family of Dark is not free from this. They are enslaved by it as well. They suffer the slings and arrows of humiliation, abandonment, rejection, pain and fear, but they use the dark forces to make them feel stronger. This allows them to run away from looking at, and admitting to, their own weakness. Family of Dark members are masters at blame and pushing away anything or anyone that they hold in judgment, and Family of Dark members are great at holding grudges.

To release yourself from those traits remember, "Forgive them, Father, they know not what they do." Strive to love unconditionally. That does not mean you condone the bad behavior as okay. It means you separate the behavior from the person doing the behavior. You try to understand the motivation behind their behavior so you can reach some level of forgiveness and move on with your life. This frees you from carrying everyone else's emotional baggage as your own, and that is essential to a happy life.

The vampire nature wants to hang on to everything and "suck it dry." To release your inner vampire nature, learn to let go, and let your God-Self steer the ship.

Clue #9 to our Empowerment: Turn and face your demons and they lose power over you. The only reason that the Dark Side has to keep you in fear is so that you don't "open the door to the closet" and discover the truth. To keep you weak the Family of Dark needs to keep you afraid, and they will do everything they can to turn you away. That is true whether considering your own personal history, or human history on a global scale.

Empowerment comes from being whole, and being whole means just that—*all of you* and *all of us*. Not just the parts we want to see. Think back on the wars that have been waged on this planet. We have been told that they were waged for a multitude of reasons, many of which we are now realizing weren't true. The Gulf of Tonkin, which got us into the Vietnam War, was a manipulated event to justify our entry into Vietnam for example. Today this is common knowledge. Yet, we still don't want to own our personal or collective shadows. Many of us have worshipped Abraham Lincoln because we were told he freed the slaves. I know I did. But, then we learned that perhaps the Civil War was really an economic war perpetrated to weaken the South, and the issue of slavery was used to justify the war. America was destroyed like it has never been destroyed before or since. It was torn apart in ways too horrible to imagine for modern Americans. It was weakened. Was industrialization already poised to do away with slavery? Did we need to kill and harm so many, including the slaves, to end slavery?

After they were released from slavery, we did little to actually help the slaves have good lives. If we were really so concerned with helping the slaves, shouldn't we have offered them much more after they were released? Shouldn't we have offered them a means to make a living? What was the real motivation behind the Civil War? I'm not answering the question, but I'm asking the questions. Certainly everyone agrees that slavery had to go, but did we ever question the destruction that brought it about? As a child I was aligned with political parties and beliefs due to my upbringing. If I had been raised in the South I might have had different beliefs drummed into me. Once again duality and division has been created. No one benefits and everyone suffers. And who does that serve?

Rethinking our history, and opening the door to our collective shadow, is essential to healing our collective karma and doing it better next time. This is exactly why the Dark Side doesn't want you to question your beliefs. It challenges their control over your consciousness.

"Question Authority" is a famous bumper sticker. Question everything you have been told if you want to begin opening the "closet doors." Most of what we believe didn't originate with us, but we bought into it hook, line and sinker.

If we admit that we don't know anything, and that most of our beliefs are cultural, we pave the way to Truth. In this way we find ourselves brave enough to see what is behind the outdated belief systems.

THE COMMON STAGES OF "AWAKENING"

Elation. The first stage of awakening is accompanied by an energetic release that feels like freedom and empowers you beyond anything you had known previously. Although there can be a shock factor to the shift that is disconcerting, and it can feel at times overwhelming, the first stage is like a rush of adrenaline to the system. If too much adrenaline is released a person can feel dizzy or have rapid heartbeats. If too much spiritual adrenaline is released a similar experience will manifest that can feel overwhelming. I'm divine! I'm immortal! I'm invincible! The soul awakens and the mind remembers who and what it really is.

Bring It On. The "bring it on" stage comes from the empowerment you feel when you become aware of your own divinity and the enormity of the soul. You feel invincible. You want to reach enlightenment quickly and painlessly; in fact, you are certain that you are only days away from it. You say to your guides and angels, "Bring it on. I can handle it." You've got it covered; until they do.

Stop! The third stage is the exhaustion phase. Suddenly everything seems to be a test. You curse the day you said, "Bring it on!" Every relationship tests your ability to be more loving. Every obstacle has a spiritual approach and a non-spiritual approach and you are overwhelmed by the tasks ahead of you. Where before you would act in a mindless manner, now you have to consider your behavior and act accordingly. Spirit seems to be testing you at every turn. Money is spiritual. Friendships are spiritual. Your car's performance is spiritual. The animals are spiritual. The trees are spiritual. The fact that you sprained your ankle is spiritual. You are overwhelmed by the thought that everything in your life is reflecting your spiritual self and you are failing miserably every time you skin your knee or your car gets a flat tire.

Life Sucks. At this point you are exhausted from trying to live up to your spiritual duties and show the world how "pure" you are, how much more spiritually evolved you are than you used to be; or than your neighbor is. You have tried to be like Jesus, Buddha, your guru or spiritual mentor, and you've failed. Didn't you yell at your children or spouse? Didn't you talk bad about a co-worker? That means you are unworthy and by projection, life is really sucky after all, so why try? You'll never get to heaven and sit with the Enlightened Masters—that's why you are here and they are on the other side of the curtain watching (and judging) you. You feel deflated.

I'm Tired of Feeling Like Crap. By stage five the glamour is gone. It appears that you have only two choices: act like a cranky, pissed-off, 3D human all the time, and bemoan your existence until you don't have any friends, or pick yourself up and dust yourself off and try to be the best person you can be by integrating some of the spiritual principles you've learned along the way. Will it get you in to see the Enlightened Masters in person or sit next to them? You have no idea. Will it make living feel better? Yes. You go for it, one day at a time, one foot in front of the other, trying to be the best person you can be.

I'm Still Here. I'm here for a reason. I have a purpose. I guess I am supposed to be in Service to God (however I choose to define it) without glamour, but with a good and open heart to the best of my ability. How may I serve?

I Get Up the Next Morning and Do the Laundry. I am always in service to my God-Self.

And finally, for those of you who are waking up to the possibility that you have incarnated on other planets I have compiled a list of what I have experienced assisting the various Starseeds to heal their karmic wounding. If it doesn't resonate with you; no problem. If it does, then great!

AN EASY TO UNDERSTAND EXPLANATION OF THE STARSEEDS

Perhaps you will recognize yourself in this list. As an angelic channel, and past life therapist, I have helped a number of Starseeds heal the karma they carried with them when they incarnated onto this planet. As a result I have seen patterns emerge among the various Starseed groups. Many souls who have been incarnating since the time of the dragons have done lives on all of these planets and more. Seekers, who study life creation with Merlin, have always experienced many different incarnations in a variety of bodies. If you are one of those you will find that you might resonate to a number of these, (and many others) depending on how much your soul template still holds the memories.

Other healers may have had different experiences; but these are mine. This list contains only a few of the Starseed possibilities. But, these are the major templates I have encountered.

Arcturians: Those who carry the Arcturian soul template are drawn to communities and they are often found in monasteries or other types of communal-spiritual living situations. In the present day they are still attracted to these communities and will often spend time living in one. If they become discouraged because the community does not meet their expectation of harmonious living, they will often go the other direction and become withdrawn.

Arcturian-humans tend to be neither dramatically attractive nor unattractive. They blend in physically to their surroundings, and do not want to draw attention to themselves. They do not like to be judged by their appearance, and they do not judge others by their appearance. Hollywood baffles them. They are kind, generous, and think first about the welfare of others. They are also the most non-sexual of the Starseeds, as the Arcturians use a non-sexual method of reproduction. So, although they do not reject sexuality, they do not seek it out.

As you remember, the Arcturians who could not raise their vibrational frequencies to the fifth or higher dimensions were cut-off from the Arcturian community and sent elsewhere. They became the Zeta Reticula Grays. Having witnessed what happened to the Zeta Reticula Grays, and how the Draconian army enslaved many of them, they question the decision to quarantine the lower vibrational Arcturians and let them fend for themselves. As a result their wounding expresses itself generally in two ways. The Arcturian elders, or those who made the vibrational lift and were not quarantined, carry guilt over the decision. Sometimes they will not allow themselves to "be all they can be." If they were an elder who participated in the decision-making to quarantine there is often some guilt attached. They might block their own happiness because they feel they do not deserve it.

If they were separated from their people and cast off, the Arcturian-human will carry rejection karma and fear. They will feel unworthy, but often be unable to discover the root cause. They may be connected to the Grays and have been visited by them in their childhood.

Both types of Arcturians have a great deal of difficulty looking at the shadow side of themselves and humanity. They don't like to see the "bad stuff," and will run away and hide from it. This is another reason the community setting appeals to them. Not only does it mimic the Arcturian lifestyle, it also provides an escape from the harshness of life.

Pleiadians: Pleiadian-humans tend to be dramatic. They are drawn to singing, dancing and other forms of creative expression. They are also drawn to nature, gardening, the fairy realm and escapism. Many of them have no problem accessing the higher dimensions and find it easier to talk to a tree than a human. Unlike Arcturians, the Pleiadians love sex. They are the ones who invented tantric sex and they understand that sex and spirituality were designed to go hand-in-hand.

They have a great deal of trouble keeping their own vibration high and are deeply impacted by the world around them. They are the empaths, and they feel the world's pain as their own. Earlier in life they will often take drugs to escape and experience a vibrational "high." This also contributes to the drama they are immersed in, and they profoundly feel all of life's ups and downs. The Pleiadian-humans who served as the Queen Bees carry profound guilt at having let their "world" down. They feel responsible for the downfall of the Pleiadian civilization and they will often punish themselves over and over as a victim—often by incarnating to very reptilian parents or marrying controlling, reptilian spouses.

There also exist a number of reptilian-Pleiadian hybrids. These are the ones who experienced the DNA experimentation after the siege of the Pleiades, and they carry both the Pleiadian and reptilian traits within them. These Starseeds struggle greatly with their inner demons.

Those that did not experience the DNA hybridization are often the more fairy-like of the Pleiadian Starseeds and they will shrink from anything that is too harsh and dark. They long to return to a world of dancing, laughing, singing and play.

Andromedans: The Andromedan-humans often work in scientific, computer, medical and other "logical" communities. If they are artists, even their art will have a scientific feel to it. Most Andromedan/humans will appear to be detached from human emotion. They observe it, but don't attach to it. They enjoy studying human behavior; but not participating in it. If you were to challenge these individuals for their detachment they would fiercely disagree with your analysis.

Once again, however, how they express themselves in those communities depends a great deal on whether they were co-opted by Vlad's army and their DNA was mixed with reptilian DNA. Because these individuals are attracted to "perfected systems" they like anything that is expressed as close to perfection as possible. They have brilliant minds and don't want to be bothered by unnecessary emotion. Unless they have reptilian DNA in them, that is. The reptilian DNA contributes to the fierce outbursts of anger and the controlling behavior that some of these humans exhibit.

The Andromedan scientists I have known also carry a great deal of personal guilt. Some of them have been running away from the work they did with the reptilian army and they tend to be self-destructive. Some are trying desperately to break their contracts with Vlad Dracula. The key to their liberation is self-love.

Alpha-Centaurians: The Alpha Centaurians that I am aware of, and have worked with, are the centaurs. As was already explained, these people will have a deep resonance for horses and will often feel most at home when with them. As a result of being divided in half the Alpha-Centaurians I have worked with tend to feel incomplete. They feel disconnected. They feel cut off from themselves and even God. They are fiercely independent and don't like to ask for help. They also tend to be mistrusting, and you can only "mess" with them once before they kick back. However, most of them (except the most cut-off and angry) are generally kind people and feel deep sorrow at the suffering of others. But, as a rule, they tend to like animals a great deal more than humans, and they feel most at home when around horses.

Sirians: Sirian-humans tend to have an air of "nobility" about them that is hard to express in words. They are powerful beings, but they have misused their power enough times that they tend to carry large karma. Many Sirians are reincarnated from the kings and rulers you read about in the Bible and ancient history. The women love jewelry and often will adorn themselves liberally. If they don't do that, then they will wear favorite pieces, usually associated with power or some magical gifts. They resonate with Ancient Egypt and have had many lives there, including lives as temple priestesses, temple priests, and other positions of authority and power.

I have noticed that many of these powerful people are running away from their own shadow, and have a great deal of difficultly looking at their past lives because their karma is enormous. If they have Annunaki blood, and were involved in the early enslavement of humanity in some way, this is particularly true. As a result many of them are in hiding.

A number of years ago I was honored to have the man who is the reincarnation of the pharaoh Akhenaten walk through my door. I had just begun doing past life therapy when he showed up. The first time I met him he was "unmasked," and his energy was so enormous I almost froze in fear. When he "unmasked" he had the large, elongated head of the Annunaki. He had unmasked to prove to me that he was who he declared himself to be. We sat and talked for a long time. It took me awhile to get over my fear of him because of this enormous energy he carried. He told me that his guides had sent him to me as I would be able to help him. When he returned for the actual session a few days later he was in full disguise and unrecognizable as the enormous energy he really was. He looked like an average Joe. Working with him to heal his karma as Akhenaten was no different than anyone else. He had suffered and was trying to heal his wounds.

In the present time his day job is unglamorous and he is truly in hiding. Sirians are not always easy to spot.

Regulans: The Regulan-humans who carry the soul memories from the multiple star system of Regulus are the large half cat, half humans depicted in the movie *Avatar*. I have only known a few of these Starseeds, but there are some similarities that emerge. Because their planet was destroyed by the robots under the command of the Andromedan scientists, these humans carry the remembrance and fear of the robot-race. They resonate deeply with the experiences of the Native Americans and the destruction of their lands. They carry wisdom of the Earth and gravitate toward natural foods, and sound healing. Much like Earth cats, they are sensual creatures who listen and feel with their entire body.

IN CONCLUSION

When we realize that both our imprisonment and our freedom are through the mind and heart, and we accept that our reality is created by our beliefs and our choices, we are more likely to choose love than hate. As stewards for Mother Earth we must begin to release ourselves from the old programs that encourage us to rape and ravage her beauty. Embracing community and releasing ourselves from the old "kill or be killed" mentality is essential for our survival. Now that we understand what has been done to us; we can undo it. Even Vlad Dracula and his demons need us to co-operate in order for them to succeed. Let's stop co-operating with him and begin to co-operate with one another. Let's choose love over fear and hate. Let's release ourselves from the Lower Matrix and remember the truth of our divine selves. As a species we have the opportunity to thrive or to destroy both ourselves and the planet we call home. Our future is truly in our hands.

Jordan Maxwell
David Icke